Columbia University

Contributions to Education

Teachers College Series

No. 729

AMS PRESS
NEW YORK

Relationship of the Professed Philosophy to the Suggested Educational Experiences

A STUDY IN CURRENT ELEMENTARY SCHOOL CURRICULUM MAKING

BY NANCY GERTRUDE MILLIGAN, Ph.D.

TEACHERS COLLEGE, COLUMBIA UNIVERSITY
CONTRIBUTIONS TO EDUCATION, NO. 729

*Published with the Approval of
Professor J. Ralph McGaughy, Sponsor*

BUREAU OF PUBLICATIONS
TEACHERS COLLEGE, COLUMBIA UNIVERSITY
NEW YORK CITY
1937

Library of Congress Cataloging in Publication Data

Milligan, Nancy Gertrude, 1889-
    Relationship of the professed philosophy to the
suggested educational experiences.

    Reprint of the 1937 ed., issued in series: Teachers
College, Columbia University. Contributions to education, no. 729.
    Originally presented as the author's thesis, Columbia.
    Bibliography: p.
    1. Education--Philosophy. 2. Education, Elementary
--Curricula. 3. Education, Elementary--Aims and
objectives. I. Title. II. Series: Columbia
University. Teachers College. Contributions to education, no. 729.

LB1570.M55 1972   372.1'9   78-177074
ISBN 0-404-55729-5

Reprinted by Special Arrangement with Teachers
College Press, New York, New York

From the edition of 1937, New York
First AMS edition published in 1972
Manufactured in the United States

AMS PRESS, INC.
NEW YORK, N. Y.   10003

Acknowledgments

I HEREIN acknowledge my indebtedness to Professor Fannie W. Dunn, Professor William Heard Kilpatrick, and Professor J. Ralph McGaughy and express deep gratitude for their valuable guidance. I am also indebted to all the members of the Elementary Education staff at Teachers College for their continued interest in this study and to the persons whose names appear under Appendix I for their co-operation from the field. To many fellow students and co-workers I am grateful for challenges and criticisms. To the Curriculum Bureau of Teachers College I wish to express appreciation for much helpful service in the use of materials.

Any possible contribution which this study may make to the enrichment of the activity program is offered in recognition of the opportunity of working with many eager children and large groups of sincere classroom teachers. I am continually grateful for the influence of a number of outstanding instructors. To those already mentioned I wish to add the names of Professor Patty Smith Hill, Professor Frederick G. Bonser, and Professor Frank M. McMurry. To the latter I am indebted for stimulation, encouragement, and valuable criticism based on observation in the field.

Contents

CHAPTER   PAGE

I. INTRODUCTION—THE CURRENT CURRICULUM SCENE AND THE
   NEED OF FURTHER INVESTIGATION   1

   The Purposes of This Study   6
   The Plan of the Research   7

II. THE ORIENTATION OF THE PERIOD OF THIS STUDY IN EDUCA-
    TIONAL THOUGHT   12

    Elements Contributing to the Educational Thought Underlying
    the Recent Curriculum Movement   14
    Forces Playing Upon the Lag in Education at the Beginning of
    the Present Century   15
    The Stirring Influence of Herbartianism   17
    The Birth of a New Psychology   18
    The Growing Influences of the Dewey Philosophy   19
    The Tests and Measurements Movement   21
    The Enriching Contribution of Industrial Arts Education....   22
    Outstanding Contributions Influencing Current Curriculum
    Thought   23
    Recent Influences on the Period of This Study   24

III. DISCUSSION OF THE FINDINGS AS THEY RESULTED FROM THE
     USE OF EACH GUIDING ELEMENT IN THE "GUIDE FOR THE
     EVALUATION OF ELEMENTARY CURRICULA"   27

     I. The Philosophy as Shown in Statements of the Point of
        View, Creeds, Aims, Objectives, and Various Plans of
        Organization   29
     II. Building the Personality as a Whole   41
     III. The Place of Environment in Learning   49
     IV. The Curriculum Maker's Theory of the Way Learning
         Takes Place   56
     V. The Place of the Teacher   67
     VI. The Choice of the Curriculum Experiences   77
     VII. The Relative Immediacy of the Experience to the Child   85
     VIII. Provision for Learning Through First-Hand Experiences   92
     IX. Provision for Creative Experience 100
     X. Growth in Intellectual Curiosity 108

v

CHAPTER   PAGE

    XI. Provision for the Enrichment of Leisure Time 116
    XII. "Socially Useful" Work 125
    XIII. Acquaintance with the National Culture for Appreciation and Improvement 131
    XIV. Provision for Growth in World-Mindedness—Building an International Interest 138
    XV. Subject matter: How Thought of and How Accordingly Used 144
    XVI. The Place of Drill 152
    XVII. The Form Used in Organizing the Curriculum Material 158
    XVIII. Some Inconsistencies Between the Philosophy and the Suggested Experiences 161
    A Summary of the Total Findings for the Several Guiding Elements 167

IV. TRENDS AS TO APPROVED POSITIONS 173

V. CONCLUSIONS, RECOMMENDATIONS, AND PROBLEMS FOR FURTHER STUDY 181

    Conclusions Which May Be Stated with a Considerable Degree of Certainty on the Basis of Evidence Found 181
    Recommendations 185
    Problems for Further Study 186

Appendix I. List of Persons Co-operating in This Study 189
Appendix II. Statements from Some of the Curriculum Makers Whose Materials Were Used 189
Bibliography 195

Chapter I

INTRODUCTION—THE CURRENT CURRICULUM SCENE AND THE NEED OF FURTHER INVESTIGATION

WHAT are we thinking on the curriculum problem? What experiences are our children having as the result of our thinking?

Our answer, revealing the inter-relationship that exists between these two encompassing phases of an outstanding educational problem, portrays with fair accuracy the program in operation in the schools of today. Our answer is a matter of major importance to the growth of the children of our country. It then becomes a question of vital significance to society as a whole.

In the area of the relationship between "curriculum-thinking" and child-experiences lies a challenging field of thought inviting continuous investigation and enrichment. Here stands the school in action reflecting a wide range of conflicting theoretical positions, contradictory experiences, and unrelated practices. Here, too, the strategic position of influence occupied by the school emphasizes its contribution to the total educative process. This institution, which has been created by a democratic society to help further the growth of a democratic type of state, carries inherently the challenge to build a better civilization.

In the on-moving stream of educational thought since the turn of the present century, few problems have appeared more steadily in the main current than some phase of this one. Many elements, to be discussed in a subsequent chapter, have poured their influence into the stream.

Even a partial survey of the current curriculum scene reveals many agencies contributing to this field. One finds a large body of curriculum literature, curriculum courses, curriculum bureaus, and curriculum laboratories. There are also curriculum studies, and curriculum committees—frequently composed of educators, parents, and laymen. Further investigation shows lists of curriculum re-

1

search in progress, curriculum conferences, and curriculum experts —subject matter and general. To this list may be added curriculum directors, curriculum budgets, many types of the so-called "curriculum set-up," and a variety and quantity of curriculum output. Remote indeed would be the situation that had not had contact with the possible services of some of these agencies. Static in the extreme would be the school that had not had its complacency affected by the general movement which these agencies reflect. This situation, then, would indicate that the far-reaching concern for the curriculum is dealing, not with a problem of minor importance, but with one that is the main current of the school's program.

For a movement as recent in the stream of educational history as the re-emphasis upon the curriculum, the widespread active interest which exists in the problem may well be credited as a gigantic stride ahead. What of the results of this interest?

A cursory examination of any segment of our curriculum output presents an interesting picture of the current thinking in this field. It runs the full gamut from an extreme right to an extreme left position in point of view and presents contradictory concepts, inconsistent suggested experiences, and conflicting practices within the various positions. One finds material ranging all the way from the stereotyped subject matter outline with its limiting end-points wholly determined in advance, to a glimpse in the current literature of the challenge to seek "desirable lines of development" worked out "in terms of *becoming* rather than in a final state of *being*." [24:374]*

Among our curriculum output it is possible to find crisp reprints of traditional subject matter outlines in use for a number of years. These are frequently prefaced by up-to-date introductions appropriating wholesale a body of objectives which have been developed upon a point of view wholly different from that incorporated in the original course. One may find records of glib quotations from a dynamic philosophy accompanied by detailed outlines of subject matter, determined wholly in advance. Such courses show many suggestions for drill of a disassociated type and as many tests as are available to insure "efficiency." There are records of venture-

---

* This and other numbers in brackets throughout the text refer to publications listed in alphabetical order in the Bibliography at the end of the book. The number after the colon refers to the page of the work cited.

some lists of "Suggested Activities" included for the frankly stated purpose of helping to "put across" subject matter previously determined. This end is said to be guaranteed by lengthy lists of drills and tests for "acquired facts." There are also records of an increasing range of "Suggested Activities" from the so-called field of social studies. Here the "tool subjects" are made safe for the learner by means of "Minimum Essentials to be Covered." In such cases the total experience is largely sealed—as to the type of outcomes—by a battery of tests. One finds an increasing number of records distinctly more inclusive of "Possible Activities" and "Activity Programs." These records reflect the influence of the activity movement upon integration and show a marked attempt to draw in more phases of the tool subjects, while at the same time they parallel their suggestions with numerous checks on the "fundamentals." Records of "Units of Work" or "Curriculum Units" appear which carry the opportunity for integration further. These latter include some excellent guiding principles for their selection, while, at the same time, they incorporate wholesale much formal textbook material and evaluate their outcomes too largely upon the latter. Among the current curriculum materials are records of "Units of Curriculum Experiences" which show that they were chosen from the learner's field of interest within guiding principles. Such experiences were selected by the teacher-pupil group and were evaluated by a better balance of all the inherent elements in the experience, although they reflected some limitation through the traditional influence of "subject matter." One discovers in a few records and in the advanced literature in the field, glimpses of the recognition of the need to clarify and extend guiding lines for the total curriculum problem. This groundwork is necessary to safeguard the possible growth for children which is inherent in rich curriculum experiences.

Most examinations of any segment of our curriculum product for the elementary schools show a small proportion of the total to be outstanding. There is a larger group which seems to reflect an early stage in the progress of a planned movement from a conservative position toward a hoped-for progressive one. However, the major portion of the curriculum output shows much evidence of clinging to a distinctly traditional position. One element they all have in common. All reflect conflicts. These conflicts seem to increase in the degree to which the instrument used, or the examiner, places emphasis upon basic elements rather than upon the mechanics of form or the manner of construction. Conflicts are to be found in the points of view held and conflicts appear within the various positions.

That confusion appears in the current curriculum thought, most persons actively engaged on the problem will admit. This confusion is not a matter of the usual healthy difference of opinion, which, capitalized constructively, may be used as an element for growth. It is increasingly apparent that the roots of this confusion penetrate deep into the problem. It has to do with conflicting points of view, conflicting practices, and concepts needing to be discarded or re-evaluated. The latter needs to be done in the light of the period in which a concept is being used rather than the period in which it came into being. These conditions create a challenging area inviting further intensive study. The investigation of crucial elements in this area may well furnish the foundation for a part of the critical thinking necessary for continuous improvement. Here lies a direct route to growth in the quality of the curriculum experiences which the school is making possible for children.

There is also apparent a tendency for the basic elements in this field not to receive the attention—except by those persons deeply concerned with the *total problem*—that is accorded to some of the more popularized but less important phases. Meanwhile, such fundamental and determining issues as the distinction between educational aims that *limit* and those that *liberate*, or the nature of experience and the part it plays in the curriculum problem frequently come in for small attention.

Were it possible to go a step beyond the present means of research and get a photostatic copy of much of the general thinking behind the curriculum picture, it is quite conceivable that an interesting condition would be portrayed. There is surface evidence of much well-seasoned conservatism, considerable honest doubt, many wavering positions, a widespread concern about the curriculum problem as a whole, and marked confusion as to wise next steps. However, it is the function of education to help guide the thinking of future generations. It must follow, therefore, that educators cannot escape the obligation to think through to a better solution some of the major problems centering around basic elements in our present curriculum thought.

If the increments of aroused interest and contributions thus far are to be capitalized, this area of existing confusion demands much investigation. This is necessary in order to clear the way for optimum growth in the field of this core problem. The location and discussion of the major conflicts should be a step toward their solution. There is need for taking soundings of the curriculum stream—in recorded results, thinking implied, suggested child experiences. There is need to see the problem as a whole with special emphasis upon the inter-relationship between our curriculum thinking and the curriculum experiences our children are having as the result of our thinking.

Participation in the educational program at any time implies some relation to this problem. Especially is this fact emphasized at the present period of the school's increasing sensitivity to change in the social terrain of which it is both part and factor—to serve and to improve. This, in turn, implies some point of view; some theoretical position held; some philosophy stated or implied. Those persons responsible for the curriculum experiences—all persons engaged in education, as well as parents and laymen to an increasing degree—add to the confusion in the current thought on the subject to the extent to which they fail to think through their particular situation collectively. This is to be done in the light of the best advanced opinion and investigations in the field before the group declares a point of view. The declared point of view is tentative to be sure. It is, however, extremely vital as a necessary compass to guide the solution of major aspects of their problem and to serve as a point of departure for further critical thinking.

For the task of thinking through this problem to a better relationship of its several elements, we may seek guidance from the field in which philosophy serves education. It is here, drawing upon philosophy both as structure and as function, that we may find assistance in formulating a theoretical position to guide the entire curriculum program. The need of an adequate theoretical background is evident in much of our curriculum product. This condition, together with the persistence of outworn concepts and a body of unrelated practices, is largely due to the lack of careful thought on the problem *as a related whole* and the statement of a guiding position arrived at. With existing conditions it is to be expected that this area should be freighted with conflicts. It would seem that here was a rich field for the services of philosophy with its ability to render aid in situations where various elements center in opposition. In evolving a guiding theoretical position as a part of our philosophy of education, we reflect a philosophy of life and the role we conceive education as playing in the growth of the individual and society as a whole. "This will involve a consideration both of the quality or value aspect of life and of the process of effecting the good life. . . . Education is here clearly implicated within life itself. We face thus in the theoretic interest an inquiry into a philosophy of life, into education as a process of self-building, and into the inter-relations of the two." [38:179]

Having evolved and stated a philosophy of education embodying a theoretical position, it follows, then, that the chief concern should be to have this guiding philosophy function consistently throughout the experiences which the school offers to children.

It is in the area of the inter-relationship between these two elements—the guiding philosophy and the resulting suggested experiences—that this study has been made. In fact the study is undertaken in the belief that the makers of any course of study will do a better piece of work and accomplish better results if they will at the outset state explicitly what guiding philosophy of curriculum making they hold and then seek consciously to apply this philosophy consistently in all they do.

The current curriculum product reflects considerable confusion in the thinking in this field. This confusion arises largely from conflicts centering about basic elements. These conflicts appear in sharp relief in the area of the inter-relationship between the guiding philosophy and the suggested experiences. The location and discussion of the underlying causes of some of these conflicts should contribute to their solution and help to enrich the school's contribution to the child's total educative process.

THE PURPOSES OF THIS STUDY

The purpose of this study was to make a critical examination of the relationship between the philosophy, stated or implied, and the corresponding suggested experiences in recent curricula for the elementary school. A further purpose was to discover, interpret, and appraise these relationships and to evaluate the means which have been used to secure them. Finally, it was the hope of the writer to locate elements and trends which contribute toward a more consistent relationship between the professed philosophy and the suggested experiences to carry out this philosophy.

In pursuit of this aim, it was essential to examine the pertinent literature in the field and to set up a comprehensive plan of research for securing, from printed curricula, the evidence upon which this study is based.

THE PLAN OF THE RESEARCH

A. *The examination of the printed curricula for public elementary schools.* The examination of the printed curricula for public elementary schools in cities of 100,000 and above, published during the period, January, 1930 to June, 1935, was made as follows: (1) "All" general courses. (2) "All" social studies courses. (3) "All" courses for one "art subject"—art. (4) "All" courses for one "tool subject"—arithmetic. ("All" is here defined in this manner: in cases where a separate course for each grade was found under either of the four preceding items, one course for the upper and one for the lower grades was used.) (5) Several courses (three to five) which seemed to be of an unusual type and published during this period. Among those chosen such titles appeared as: "Nutrition for the Elementary School Grades," "A Healthy Personality for Home, School, and Community," and "Vacation Schools." One recent state course was included. (6) Several courses (three to five) "General" or "Social Studies," published for the public elementary schools in cities smaller than 100,000. This last-named group was chosen from lists of courses judged by the Curriculum Bureau at Teachers College to be outstanding. They were recent but not limited to the January, 1930, to June, 1935, period. This last phase of the plan is in recognition of some of the valuable contributions that have come from smaller school systems.

B. *The development of A Guide for the Evaluation of Elementary School Curricula.* (1) Bases for the tentative selection of the guiding elements incorporated in the guide were: (a) lists of guiding elements; (b) personal experience in the field; (c) advice of experts; (d) approval and advice of guiding committee. (2) Evaluation and extension of the guiding elements through group judgment.

For this important phase of the study the tentative list of guiding elements was prepared and presented to three representative groups of persons in education. The following requests were made: (1) Check those you would exclude for lack of value. (2) Allowing for some expected overlapping, check those you would exclude for this reason. (3) Add other guiding elements which you consider pertinent to the problem. (4) Have you participated in some phase of curriculum construction during the past seven years? All activities concerned with the experiencing and recording of further worthwhile curriculum material or the trying out of suggested experiences were to be interpreted as curriculum construction.

Three representative elementary education groups were used for the final judging of the guiding elements. These were: the Major Course in Elementary Education, Teachers College; a Course for Elementary School Principals; and an Elementary Seminar of the same department. All reactions from persons who had not participated in some phase of curriculum. construction during the time mentioned were eliminated from the summary. The guiding elements thus obtained were defined and incorporated into a guide devised for use in making "A Study of the Relationship between the Philosophy and the Suggested Experiences in Recent Printed Curricula for the Elementary School." There is no claim that the guiding elements used are all-inclusive in the field, but it is maintained that a number of the major elements pertinent to the problem were selected and incorporated into the Guide. Each guiding element used and its findings will be discussed in Chapter III of this study.

C. *Group evaluation of the guide and its use.* (1) The guiding elements used were objectified by their application to suggested learning experiences as the guide was tried out, by individual use, in the examination of curricula. (2) An evaluation was made, both of the guide and of the examiner's individual evaluation of curriculum material obtained through its use. This was done by securing group reaction (five to seven) to the same course of study. The persons used for this phase of the research were selected for the following reasons: (a) interest in the same field of education;

(b) background of experience; (c) the reflection of much of the same philosophy of education as that held by the writer; (d) regional distribution for the country at large.

Summaries of the findings on this jury judgment agreement will be made for each guiding element used. They will appear in the appropriate succeeding sections.

D. *Statements from a few curriculum makers whose courses were used in the study.* These statements were requested from curriculum makers whose material reflected more consistency than usual. Their reaction was requested to two elements in the problem: first, their point of view on the importance of the relationship between the philosophy and the suggested experiences; second, how they obtained the relationship reflected in their printed curricula.

These further elements functioned in the research for this study. The time placement—January, 1930, to June, 1935—seemed most likely to be of service to the curriculum problem. The lists obtainable from curriculum bureaus for the period used showed more publications from cities of the size chosen than from smaller cities. This condition was probably influenced by the prevailing economic situation. On account of the size of the field, it was necessary to have such a study concentrate upon some type of situation. Since as extensive and recent a view of the curriculum scene as possible was desired, the type of situation having the most published material was used. The last Census Report showed 93 cities of the size chosen for use in this study. Notwithstanding the prevailing conditions, available lists showed that approximately 40 per cent of this group published material during this period. Courses available through the curriculum bureaus were used. Although these centers continually seek to keep their material up to date by requesting copies of new publications, it is quite possible that material was produced which was not sent in. No claim is herein made for the examination of such material. Where the element of choice entered into the selection of material for the special phases mentioned, a regional distribution for the country as a whole was kept in mind.

A total of 71 courses of study was examined.

The foregoing plan of research, together with group evaluation of the guiding elements used, group evaluation of the examiner's findings through the use of the guide, and statements from selected curriculum makers whose materials were used, is the foundation upon which this study is based. It was concluded that the sources used would furnish sufficiently representative and ample data from which interpretations and reliable conclusions might be made.

The writer is well aware that the printed curricula may give an inadequate picture of the school's program in action. A number of elements enter here. By the very nature of experience, its dynamic qualities are largely dependent upon environmental factors, so that records and suggestions cannot reasonably be expected to carry a total picture of the possible richness of suggested experience-situations. Conflicts in major elements, as previously discussed, cause numerous inconsistencies both in the printed material and in the apparent gaps between it and the program in action. Elements which contribute to this latter situation are the usual valuable group of outstanding teachers who guide children in many worth-while experiences despite formal curricula. This gap between the school in action and the suggested curriculum experiences is further increased by the too frequent static interpretation of suggestions rich in content. A curriculum program in which there is too rapid advance to allow time for healthy growth has added to the gap and to the general confusion. So-called curriculum experts without the experience necessary for a laboratory point of view in the field for which they are making recommendations are adding to the confusion. Limiting situations preventing the quality of contribution to the total problem that is inherent in the services of those guiding the program often occur. Some programs suggested to serve large areas, such as state courses, require adjustment to local conditions. Further discrepancy arises from the failure of many leaders to work toward a collectively determined guiding philosophy—somewhat in advance of the present situation—and a wholesome co-operative attempt to interpret this philosophy into action. Such a procedure would include critical thinking to improve results. It is to be expected that such conditions would produce a gap between printed curricula and the school's program. This condition will continue until a more dynamic concept of the curriculum is evolved, promoting relationships and making possible more meaningful experiences.

However, the increasing need for seeing the curriculum problem as a related whole and the fact that it is not feasible to approach a study of this scope from the laboratory angle make it reasonable to assume that recent printed curricula reflect some philosophy— stated or implied—and offer suggestions for possible experiences to carry out that philosophy. The inter-relationship shown between these two phases of the problem will be a fairly safe reflection of the current curriculum thinking. This study deals with this relationship as found in the printed curricula.

The attempt has been made, through the guide devised for the study of this relationship, to approach the problem by seeking important guiding elements rather than through an atomistic analysis of subject matter content. The point of view of any curriculum maker on these guiding elements reveals to a large extent the philosophy which he holds and which should appear in "Statements of the Point of View," "Creed," "Aims," and "Various Plans of Organization." The consistency with which the philosophy, stated or implied, has been carried out should be revealed by its embodiment in the program of suggested experiences. "What will it profit a man to do this, that, and the other specific thing if he has no clear idea of why he is doing them, no clear idea of the end to be reached?" [21:7]

The guide used for collecting the data upon which this study is based made provision for various theoretical positions. For the writer education is growth—taking place through the continuous reconstruction of individual and social experience.

The problem herein discussed is a study of the relationship between the philosophy, stated or implied, and the suggested experiences to carry out this philosophy, as found in recent printed curricula for the elementary school.

Chapter II

THE ORIENTATION OF THE PERIOD OF THIS STUDY IN EDUCATIONAL THOUGHT

IN ORDER to be effective for future guidance, any analysis of the curriculum thinking for the period under discussion in this study must, in turn, recognize the relationship of this chosen period to the educational background out of which it came into being. The curriculum present must acknowledge its indebtedness to what has gone before, and be sensitive to the major influences which have contributed to the current thinking in the field.

In the on-moving stream of educational thought since the turn of the present century, many forces have poured their influence into this period. In the last decade preceding the new century, the growing controversy centering about both the curriculum content and long-accepted practices gave promise of an awakening interest of unusual scope. This increasing challenge of the educational status quo was inevitable. It accrued as the result of the changing economic and social conditions, and caused the healthy questioning of long regimentation and lag in the inherited educational program.

This interest has outstripped its early promise. It has increased both in range and in quality to the stage where the need of curriculum improvement is recognized as a major educational responsibility of nation-wide proportions. During the first three decades of the century and reaching back into the nineties the up-building of the curriculum interest was notably influenced, and the nature of the movement at various periods was reflected by a series of reports. Outstanding among these were: the Reports of the National Committees, Reports of the National Herbartian Society—1893-1901, and a series of Reports of Research Studies. The National Committee on the Economy of Time was organized in 1911 for four years' work. These reports appeared in the *Yearbooks* of the National Society for the Study of Education from 1915 to 1919.

During this period the Department of Superintendence of the National Education Association initiated a series of nation-wide co-operative studies. They were prepared by a National Commission and the research staff of the Association in Washington, D. C. The results of these studies appeared in the *Yearbooks* of this group from 1925 to 1929. All these studies and reports left their distinct imprint upon the curriculum content of the period and influenced subsequent educational thought. According to some authorities the early reports of the National Committees were not always based upon sound educational philosophy. They did not see the curriculum problem as a whole, and the emphasis which they placed upon isolated subjects had a marked tendency to prolong the conditions which leaders in education were trying to break down.

In these years of rapid change several outstanding curricula, to be discussed later, were produced and the beginnings of a few of the early curriculum programs of planned duration were started on their way. Near the end of the first quarter of the century the group of advanced thinkers responsible for the *Twenty-Sixth Yearbook* of the National Society for the Study of Education devoted their efforts to meeting an apparent need of the curriculum problem and made history in this field. Their sincere attempt to get together on a composite statement of a body of curriculum principles produced results, which, together with other potent elements included in this contribution, served as a landmark to guide further curriculum efforts.

At practically the same time as this notable contribution of curriculum principles, the *Fourth Yearbook* of the Department of Superintendence of the National Education Association further contributed to the interest in the curriculum problem. It presented a condensed view of the various school subjects and reports of the current research in the field. It also re-emphasized the position taken by the group previously mentioned that the curriculum problem was a continuous one and should be provided for as such. The publication of this group saw "The Nation at Work on the Curriculum for the Public Schools." Between this event and the time when the effects of the prevailing economic conditions became apparent in the field of education, the curriculum output reached its peak as to quantity.

ELEMENTS CONTRIBUTING TO THE EDUCATIONAL THOUGHT
UNDERLYING THE RECENT CURRICULUM MOVEMENT

What of the educational thought giving birth to this widespread curriculum interest? To what many-faceted major influences is the period under discussion in this study indebted?

In seeking this answer let us examine the high points in the educational thought most directly contributing to the five-year period chosen for study. From 1930 back to the beginning of the present century is a comparatively brief time-span in the history of education. Nevertheless these years are reputed to be very crucial ones in American educational thought. In 1924 Suzzallo wrote:

> The quarter of a century just passed encompasses no ordinary years in the history of education. It was the most extraordinary period in American educational development. No similar span of time in America or elsewhere has covered such important changes in the philosophy, the science, and the practice of school administration and school teaching. It was ushered in by the stimulating discussion of foreign educational philosophies which American students of education brought home from Germany. The United States lost for the time being that provincial and traditional point of view which had characterized its pedagogical thinking since the Civil War, at least so far as the most influential educational theorists were concerned. Experimentation on the basis of deductions from new assumptions and premises characterized many school systems. The self-satisfied stolidity of traditional American practice was broken. [71:xii]

What wonder that these years should give evidence of being "no ordinary years in the history of education"? Were they not heir to a century of gigantic achievements and their resulting problems— a century in which the frontier was pushed to the Pacific? The physical barriers of a continent were mastered. The Union was preserved. Unparalleled transportation was developed. A continuing problem of poorly regulated immigration—of such magnitude as history has nowhere else recorded—confronted America. The colossal problems resulting from too rapid urbanization, in the change from an agrarian to an industrial nation, were steadily forced into the foreground. And, commanding the respect of the world, provision for the ever-present desire for education had been cemented into the foundation of the national structure through the principle of universal education at public expense.

These years were the century's heir both to the first stages of the material security which young nations must achieve for themselves in order to exist and to many pressing social changes that have had a long struggle to find recognition in the curriculum programs serving the period. Writing on the curriculum problem of that day, Dewey takes the position that educational problems and movements are a reflection of social changes.

The marked tendency of the time was for the program in operation within the school to reflect little or no connection with the life outside the school. That condition is here defined, for further use, as lag. This apparent lag in education seemed to be largely due to traditional encrustment, length of time usually required for such an undertaking as any degree of reconstruction in fundamental principles, and the numerous social and economic elements feeding into the situation and causing rapid change in the social order which the educational program was attempting to serve. And, finally, the most fundamental element in this condition arose from the fact that education in this country had inherited its point of view and its procedure, to a large degree, from the Old World. Consequently, it carried on in a social structure unlike that which it had been shaped to serve.

It is, then, not surprising that when the American educational program of a period of such rapidly increasing complexity of economic and social conditions was considered in the light of its total service it should reflect much lag. Writing in 1926, Dr. Harold Rugg says on the problem of lag:

A century and a half of American independence have been marked by the development of two parallel but rarely merging currents: One, the overwhelming human torrent, . . . the other, the sluggish stream of education. [51:8]

. . . The public school has lagged far behind. It has never caught up with the momentum of industry, business, community life, or politics. Only rarely has it succeeded in dealing with contemporary issues and conditions: never has it anticipated social needs. [51:4]

FORCES PLAYING UPON THE LAG IN EDUCATION AT THE BEGINNING OF THE PRESENT CENTURY

Two sources of influence were playing upon this evident state of lag in education behind the social needs of the period. First, those forces inherent in the social-economic structure itself, outside the then accepted field of education, which were both the cause and the result of the rapid change apparent in this period; second, the advanced thinkers within the educational field itself. Cubberley writes of a part of this "extraordinary period in American educational development":

> Two camps opposed each other during this period. . . . One camp represented the older point of view, advocated the status quo, and desired standardization, uniformity, and organized methods of teaching. The other camp . . . advocated flexibility, more individualized instruction, and an enrichment of the curriculum based on the normal activities of the child. [12:539]

The new century opened with many problems and a promising inheritance of educational thought and leadership. From the latter years of the preceding century and carrying over into the new, there was an interesting combination of forces and reformers. All these elements produced the ferment which called forth much critical thinking. Out of this condition progress was started all along the educational line.

Present-day analysts of current educational thought and procedure are well accustomed to weighing various elements in terms of their possible contribution to the development of the child. The fact that child-growth now receives the major emphasis in educational thought and that the program to serve this end is, in theory at least, under continuous study, stands out today. This condition is the result of reforms having their beginning back in these changing years.

Among the contributions enriching education, preceding and into the new century, was that of Francis W. Parker. All records of his work indicate that he was an educator of unusual vision. He was an idealist and had a rare understanding of child nature. As an outstanding nonconformist to the grip of regimentation of his time, he possessed the ability of converting his theoretical ideas into rich experiences for children. Through study in Germany he had freed himself of the prevailing traditional thought in American education. In the "Quincy New Departure," Cook County Normal School, and in Chicago University School he aroused much interest in the results he achieved through his understanding of child nature. He experimented at a period of marked regimentation largely dominated by the faculty psychology. However, he cut through traditional school subject divisions, stressed first-hand experiences served by subjects as a related whole, and provided a rich learning environment giving the child's natural tendencies opportunity for self-expression. It is said that Parker was greatly influenced by the underlying spirit and truths of the kindergarten and sought to carry them over, as far as practical, into the elementary school. His contribution of an enriched curriculum-content revealed in the laboratory of the classroom had a wide influence upon subsequent educational thought and practice.

Contemporary with the work of Parker, while at Chicago, were the scholarly achievements of President G. Stanley Hall. To him current educational thought is indebted for his pioneering in the child-study movement, his emphasis upon the study of psychology for its practical services to education, his contribution to the psychology of adolescence, and his early records of observations. These and his other contributions helped to introduce the scientific element into the study of education. Both Hall and Parker contributed to the foundation interest in making education a subject of study.

THE STIRRING INFLUENCE OF HERBARTIANISM

One of the most dynamic educational influences which the new century inherited was that of Herbartianism. The nineties witnessed its introduction and experienced the first impact of its stimulating thought.

Among the forces that affected the American school . . . none is to be mentioned with higher respect than the influences which originated with a German psychologist and educator, John Frederick Herbart. It was to Rein's seminar [professor of pedagogics at the University of Jena] that a number of young American students were attracted, of whom the best known were Edmund James, Charles De Garmo, and the brothers, Charles and Frank McMurry. These young men brought to this country the Herbartian theories and practices in the early 'nineties and led a spirited campaign for their adoption in the common school. [61:414]

This new body of educational thought emphasized the doctrines of apperception and interest, the culture-epoch theory, and the five formal steps. Into an educational structure influenced by the faculty psychology and highly dominated by the traditionally unrelated way of handling subject matter these new elements were introduced. Apperception excluded mere acquisition of facts. Meanings had to be built up to develop relationships and organize ideas into a related experience. The resulting concept formed the center of instruction. ". . . the Herbartians insisted that the subject-matter of instruction should consist of 'methodical unities,' or thought units, or units of instruction." [61:474] The emphasis upon interest in the Herbartian pedagogy excluded externally imposed tasks. Mere information did not suffice. Interest was many-sided. "Experience" and "social intercourse" were held to be the sources of interests. The five formal steps were widely accepted in teacher-training centers. The culture-epoch theory brought enlivening materials to the curriculum, especially in the lower grades. The Herbartians cut through the unrelated way of handling school subjects by their insistence that the materials of instruction should be organized according to meanings. This caused a movement for the elimination of useless material in the curriculum. They exerted .a great influence upon the technique of teaching and the organization of the curriculum. "Attacking squarely, as this movement did, so much of what then prevailed it brought conscious attention to almost the whole range of theory regarding the educative process." [40:61]

THE BIRTH OF A NEW PSYCHOLOGY

During this vital pre-century decade a new psychology entered the educational thought stream. This contribution by William James was an important event in education. It was the beginning of the new psychology in this country and took its fundamental point of view from the Darwinian theory of evolution. Paralleled by the rising philosophy of the period—each enriching the other—it contributed to giving a new turn to the study of education. This biological psychology meant changes in concepts regarding the fundamental processes of education. Again, through Darwin's doctrine of evolution, the field of biology served educational thought.

At this period in American education there was an interesting state of confusion regarding the psychological assumptions upon which the curriculum experiences and the teaching practices were based. The faculty psychology largely prevailed in the teacher-training centers and colleges. The associationist psychology of Herbart was accepted as the basis of the teachings of the enthusiastic leaders whose influence was being felt all along the educational line. The kindergarten group followed the psychology inherent in the teachings of Froebel. Into this psychological scene the new biological psychology was started on its way. From the time of this important contribution the biological basis rather than the metaphysical was winning its way in American psychological thought. Experimentation and observation of the actual responses of the child were emphasized. James's *Principles of Psychology* and his *Talks to Teachers* had a marked influence upon educational thought.

It is, however, in the work of Thorndike that educational psychology first takes form as a consistent and relatively well-rounded body of knowledge, based on experimentation and observation, and having always as its final basis of reference the actual behavior of a human being undergoing the stimulus of a definite situation. . . . Thorndike's is, in every sense, the outstanding name in modern educational psychology. [42:105]

Thorndike's *Educational Psychology*, in three volumes, written during the years 1903 to 1913, made history in the field. It has been called a collection of principles and a handbook of practices. This and the numerous contributions which followed from the same author have been one of the outstanding influences in a generation of educational thought.

THE GROWING INFLUENCES OF THE DEWEY PHILOSOPHY

Rising to prominence in the nineties and steadily increasing to its far-reaching influence of the present period, the democratic philosophy of Professor John Dewey has become the core of frontier educational thought in America and has exerted considerable influence abroad. Dewey has led in the development of the philosophy of education in this country and through him and other outstanding proponents the democratic ideal—as opposed to the ideal of aristocracy—has been continuously voiced for the service of education. He made his school at Chicago University an educational laboratory—"a laboratory of applied psychology"—as he sought to work out a program rich in opportunity for the child to practice "social living."

One reason certainly for the great influence of Dewey's educational theory in this country is that this theory made a serious attempt to understand and to clarify the meaning of the democratic movement. In Dewey's theory enrichment of experience and preparation for membership in a democratic social order are brought together in a unified program. For Dewey all educational thinking leads back to the meaning of social. [4:29]

Dewey's theories were based on the new biological psychology of William James. Educational thought had received a new and transforming element in the conception of behavior as reaction to situation. Early in the century the need for activity was placed on a new basis. In Dewey's continuous effort to uproot the outworn patterns of thought and to advance the democratic philosophy of education his writings were considered epoch-making contributions to the field.

It has been well for the democratic philosophy of education that the contribution of Professor William H. Kilpatrick entered the stream of educational thought during the second decade of the century. He has interpreted the underlying principles advocated by Dewey to large groups of teachers and parents by applying these principles all along the educational line. He has given living dimensions to the part experience plays in the educative process. His digest of "The Project Method," based upon Dewey's conception of the complete act of thought, has had a wide influence toward a less formal elementary school. The democratic philosophy of education has been advanced by his writings, in a number of which he has courageously and consistently applied its doctrines and ideals to present-day social conditions. His *Education for a Changing Civilization* is considered a classic in this field. He has created a new challenge for education in its service to society through his vision of the role it may play in building a better social order. Rugg, in 1926, wrote of this contribution:

During the past ten years a new and rigorous impetus has been given to the dissemination of the doctrine of educational growth through the work of William H. Kilpatrick. During that time, through several publications and conspicuous success with thousands of students in Teachers College, Professor Kilpatrick has exerted a wide-spread influence on the vitalizing of elementary-school instruction. Kilpatrick has assembled and presented to teachers more concretely than any other worker the essential principles underlying the philosophy of growth through creative experience. He has integrated into a systematic philosophy of educational method the essential ideas of biological evolution and of dynamic psychology as developed by James, Thorndike, and others. [51:103]

The doctrine of education as growth through the continuous reconstruction of individual and group experience is one of the foremost tenets in educational thought and serves as a compass to guide much of the recent curriculum thinking.

THE TESTS AND MEASUREMENTS MOVEMENT

Another major influence affecting the curriculum problem has been the tests and measurements movement. Counting and the evaluation of the objective appeared in educational procedure near the close of the century. The testing and measurement movement has grown from infancy to maturity during the last three decades. Few influences on the curriculum content have been more marked than this one. This movement has made a contribution both in content and in scientific procedure. The work of a number of outstanding leaders in this field has been far-reaching. In some phases of its application it has produced results which need further careful study by all persons interested in education. It has promoted a type of school organization, based upon so-called ability grouping, which is being increasingly questioned for results considered of larger value than a claimed subject matter efficiency. It has tended to over-emphasize the testable elements of the curriculum and thus to deter recognition of other vital values of the total experience-situation. More "efficient" results from the use of outworn traditional theories and practices have received the major emphasis in many educational programs rather than the examination and re-evaluation of these theories for their service as a guide to the selection of rich experiences for the growing child.

From a check on so-called subject matter efficiency to the determination of educational objectives, the tests and measurements movement with its emphasis on the "scientific" approach has affected the curriculum problem all along the line. That the materials of this movement need extension and improvement leaders in the field are frank to admit. That there are areas in which negative results have accrued from the movement most students of education are well aware. This condition arises largely from these factors: the frequent misapplication of a new tool; the too widely prevalent concept that so-called subject matter test results constitute the most important, or the sole, criterion of efficiency in an educational program presuming to function in the lives of children. On this important phase of the curriculum problem Bode says:

The danger in the enthusiasm for the "scientific" determination of objectives in education lies in the fact that it obscures the need of breaking from the old standards and old ideals. [4:40]

THE ENRICHING CONTRIBUTION OF INDUSTRIAL ARTS EDUCATION

An enriching contribution of a unique type quietly made itself felt in educational thought during these years under discussion. Industrial arts education, under the far-seeing leadership of the late Professor Bonser, utilized and made more meaningful the things of everyday life, making life at hand more meaningful and more likely of further enrichment. Here, indeed, was education as life itself. Food, clothing, and shelter were used as starting points; here were important life issues. Whether in the use of the immediate or in the study of the past, education to Professor Bonser meant the finding and using of new meanings for the enrichment of daily life. His work at Cheney, Washington, Macomb, Illinois, and Teachers College, Columbia University, New York, gave evidence of his philosophy in action. The Speyer School Curriculum, developed with his co-workers over a period of two years, appeared in 1912 and was considered an epoch-making production in the field. Early in the movement he set a precedent for co-operative curriculum making. "Far more than is usual, the individual grade teachers and supervisers have had a responsible share in the suggestion, selection or exclusion, and organization of material." [6:iii] This publication, Professor Bonser's *Elementary School Curriculum*, and his writings in the field of industrial arts have had an enriching influence on current curriculum thought.

Many contributors, besides those discussed in the preceding passages, have influenced the present thinking in this field. Among others the names of Bagley, Bobbit, Bode, Charters, Collings, Counts, Horn, Judd, Meriam, and Rugg are outstanding. In point of view they represent the full range in position—in some phase of their thinking—from the extreme right to the extreme left. Each has contributed to this important problem from his particular position.

OUTSTANDING CONTRIBUTIONS INFLUENCING
CURRENT CURRICULUM THOUGHT

Among the many contributions affecting the curriculum, from the turn of the century to the period chosen for this study, several have been especially significant. They have been valuable for their educational message and their contribution to the conflict of thought out of which progress is made. A few are as follows: Dewey: *School and Society, The Child and the Curriculum, How We Think, Interest and Effort, Democracy and Education;* Bagley: *Classroom Management, The Educative Process, Determinism in Education;* Mc-Murry: *Elementary School Standards;* Kilpatrick: *The Project Method, The Foundations of Method, Education for a Changing Civilization;* Bonser: *The Elementary School Curriculum;* Bonser and Mossman: *Industrial Arts for the Elementary School;* Lincoln School Staff: *Curriculum Making in an Elementary School;* Meriam: *Child Life and the Curriculum;* Rugg and Shumaker: *The Child Centered School;* Bobbit: *How to Make a Curriculum;* Bode: *Modern Educational Theories;* Charters: *Curriculum Construction;* Collings: *An Experiment with a Project Curriculum;* Hopkins: *Curriculum Principles and Practices.*

A number of group contributions were made. The following have been effective both in shaping curriculum thought and in determining so-called subject matter. "The Report of the Committee on Curriculum," presented in the *Twenty-Sixth Yearbook* of the National Society for the Study of Education, has had a far-reaching influence. Its composite statement, by the leaders forming the committee, gave a body of guiding principles to serve the total problem and its records of work in the field gave new impetus to the movement. Later *Yearbooks* of this society have published Reports of Committees on "Nature and Nurture"; "Arithmetic"; "Rural Education and Textbooks in Education"; "Science"; "Teaching Geography"; "The Activity Movement." Other publications of influence have been: Reports of the National Committees; Reports of Department of Supervisors and Directors of Instruction of the National Education Association; *Yearbooks* of the Department of Superintendence. The reports of these groups and the Research Bulletins for the last decade reflect emphasis upon the curriculum problem. The *Fourteenth Yearbook*, 1936, reports on "The Social Studies Curriculum." All these reports have influenced this problem.

Another forceful influence on curriculum thought throughout this period has come from two sources: first, the early epoch-making curricula published in the field; second, an increasing number of curriculum programs initiated with the definite intent of considering the curriculum problem as a continuous one. These have published their results largely during the last decade. The first phase of this influence came from the laboratory schools. Among the early results, the curriculum developed at the Cook County Normal School by Parker and the Speyer School Curriculum guided by Professor Bonser were outstanding. The Baltimore County Curriculum made history in its field. The *Twenty-Sixth Yearbook* records the following laboratory schools as contributing to the problem: The Experimental Laboratory School, University of Chicago; Lincoln School of Teachers College; Iowa State University Laboratory School; University of Missouri Experimental School; Horace Mann School at Teachers College. The second phase of this influence has centered in public school systems and has been effective during the past decade in promoting the curriculum movement on a large scale. While many programs exist throughout the country as a whole, some of the larger school systems which have reports recorded in the *Twenty-Sixth Yearbook* are as follows: Burlington, Iowa; Denver, Colorado; Detroit, Michigan; Los Angeles, California; St. Louis, Missouri. All have contributed vitally to their particular curriculum problem and have made varying contributions to point the way for further large-scale efforts. Among the outstanding programs that of Denver, under the guidance of Superintendents Newlon and Threlkeld, has received wide recognition. One of its central tenets has been teacher participation. On a principle so fundamental to progressive growth as this one, the Denver emphasis has been epoch-making. "Since teaching is a professional job, the practitioner can be master of his profession only if he is conversant with the theories that he practices." [51:233]

RECENT INFLUENCES ON THE PERIOD OF THIS STUDY

The pressure of rapidly changing social and economic conditions surrounding the educational program through this period, and the

leaven in the educational thought within the group set the stage
for the curriculum movement to go forward at an increasing tempo,
when it was once well started. "Prior to 1925 fewer than 1500
courses of study had been published in the United States. In the
last ten years more than 35,000 have been produced." [50:344]
These figures, attained in spite of the limitations of economic conditions during a portion of this ten-year period, give an idea of the
quantity of the curriculum product. Only much careful investigation and evaluation can even approximately determine its *quality.*

Parallel with the increasing tempo of curriculum production a
number of elements more recently emphasized have fed their contributions into the educational thought stream and influenced the
curriculum thinking of the five-year period used in this study.

The Activity Movement grows apace. It embodies some of the
basic elements in the preceding Project Method and reflects possibilities of a growing contribution through its concept that education is inherent in rich and intelligent living with increasing self-
direction. This applies to the social heritage and to present efforts
for the improvement of future living. Between the whole-hearted
acceptance of its proponents and the criticism of its opponents,
this movement should be improved and guided for its possible wide
service to child development through the enrichment of the total
educative experience. The Progressive Education Movement steadily gains under its declaration of intention to create better growing
conditions for children by escaping from the formalism of the old
type of school. All the while it is increasingly aware of the need
to further define underlying principles and clarify current practices. The Scientific Movement has exerted a wide influence. It is
being shaped for further service through the criticism it has received. Some of this is due to the misuse of tests in preserving the
traditional subject matter point of view in education and frequent
over-emphasis upon the "scientific approach" to the exclusion of
other elements in dealing with problems of human relationships. A
number of influences are swinging the emphasis away from the
atomistic treatment of life in the field of psychology. The Gestalt
Movement adds to other contributions in stressing the reaction of
the organism as a whole. This tendency has far-reaching implications for the educational field.

Into the forging of the educational thought from the turn of the century to the period of this study many contributions have poured their influence. The frontier efforts of Parker to break away from the pattern of the old regimented school and the valuable work of Hall in starting the child-study movement were outstanding. The challenge of the Herbartians to the entire educative process was one of the invigorating influences. The revolutionary psychology of James and the steadily increasing influence of the Dewey philosophy contributed to the foundations of educational thought. The Tests and Measurement Movement and the growing tendency to question the use of the "scientific" method are important issues. The influence of "Object Teaching," "Units of Thought," the Project Method, the Activity Movement, and Curriculum Units reflect the current educational thought of the periods. The increasing tendency to swing from an atomistic to an organismic treatment of human behavior is vital. The evaluation of proposed curriculum experiences for their "social values" is a fundamental gain. The influence of the perplexing social and economic conditions of the period challenge education to assume a more dynamic role.

Such are the many-faceted influences to which the curriculum thought of the period of this study falls heir. If history runs true to its former records the educational resurgence that is to follow the present depression must take stock of a number of elements. The nation-wide curriculum interest will go forward. The movement will take on the element of a critical examination of itself. It will study its past, carefully evaluate its present, enrich its future.

Chapter III

DISCUSSION OF THE FINDINGS

As They Resulted from the Use of Each Guiding Element in the "Guide for the Evaluation of Elementary Curricula"

It has been mentioned previously that this attempt to approach the problem of curriculum evaluation would be made by seeking important guiding elements rather than through an atomistic analysis of so-called subject matter content. It is herein maintained that the curriculum maker's point of view on these guiding elements should reveal, to a large extent, the philosophy which he holds. It is reasonable, also, to expect his professed philosophy to appear in "Statements of the Point of View," "Creeds," "Aims," "Objectives," and "Various Plans of Organization." The consistency with which this philosophy has been carried out should be revealed by its embodiment in the experience-situations which are suggested in the printed curricula.

It is the conviction of the writer that the approach to the problem of curriculum evaluation which is used in this study liberates possibilities for the enrichment of all curriculum experiences. These guiding elements should help in the appraisal of present curricula. They should assist in selecting the type of possible experiences—rather than a particular experience—where suggestions are made in advance. Most important of all, they should serve as tentative guiding lines to insure balance and richness where the curriculum experiences are largely determined in progress.

The important guiding elements selected for the evaluation of curriculum materials and incorporated in the guide used for collecting the findings for this study were determined as described in Chapter I. Each of these guiding elements appears in the various sections of this chapter together with the results obtained from its application to curriculum materials. The guiding elements selected and discussed are as follows:

27

The Philosophy as Shown in Statements of the Point of View, Creeds, Aims, Objectives, and Various Plans of Organization.
Building the Personality as a Whole.
The Place of Environment in Learning.
The Curriculum Maker's Theory of the Way Learning Takes Place.
The Place of the Teacher.
The Choice of the Curriculum Experiences.
The Relative Immediacy of the Experience to the Child.
Provision for Learning through First-Hand Experiences.
Provision for Creative Experience.
Growth in Intellectual Curiosity.
Provision' for the Enrichment of Leisure Time.
"Socially Useful" Work.
Acquaintance with the National Culture for Appreciation and Improvement.
Provision for Growth in World-Mindedness—Building an International Interest.
Subject Matter: How Thought of and How Accordingly Used.
The Place of Drill.
The Form Used in Organizing the Curriculum Material.
Some Inconsistencies between the Philosophy and the Suggested Experiences.

It seems well to re-emphasize here that no claim is made that the foregoing guiding elements are all-inclusive in the evaluation of curriculum experience. However, it is maintained that a number of the major elements pertinent to the problem have been selected. As mentioned elsewhere, these guiding elements were incorporated in "A Guide for the Evaluation of Elementary School Curricula" and applied, as outlined in the plan of research.

From the point of view of the writer no guiding element exists isolated from the background of relationship uniting it with sensitive balance to the total body of elements used. While attention is concentrated upon a single element in the following discussions, its various relationships are kept in mind so that it functions as an integral part of the curriculum problem as a whole.

In the collection and discussion of the findings on these various guiding elements, effort has been made to keep the thread of the core problem—the relationship between the professed philosophy and the suggested educational experiences—consistently at the focus of attention. The philosophy has been revealed through the point of view of the curriculum maker on all the guiding elements, but especially from statements under the element dealing with the philosophy. The suggested experiences have appeared under all the guiding elements, but especially under the element dealing with subject matter. Each course was examined not only for the various aspects defined under a particular guiding element but also for the point of view of that course under the element dealing with the philosophy, and the position of the course under subject matter, as set up for that guiding element.

The main aspects set up for these two guiding elements—the one dealing with the professed philosophy, the other with the suggested educational experiences—should be kept in mind. The former is discussed in the next section. Since the latter appears near the end of the proposed list, the positions set up under "Subject Matter: How Thought of and How Accordingly Used" are here stated as a possible aid to the reader:

1. Subject-matter-set-out-to-be-learned.
2. Subject matter largely predetermined but enlivened by various activities.
3. Subject matter as a means to an end.
4. Subject matter as the total experience.

I. THE PHILOSOPHY AS SHOWN IN STATEMENTS OF THE POINT OF VIEW, CREEDS, AIMS, OBJECTIVES, AND VARIOUS PLANS OF ORGANIZATION

As Characterized in the "Guide for the Evaluation of Elementary Curricula" and Found Through Its Use

What is the professed philosophy which has been used to guide the making of this course as found in: 1. Statements of the Point of View. 2. Creeds. 3. Aims. 4. Objectives. 5. Plan of Organization.

Some ways through which the curriculum maker's professed philosophy appeared in the 71 courses examined.

Ways the Professed Philosophy Appeared: Courses
  1. Statements of the Point of View   31
  2. Creeds   8
  3. Aims   18
  4. Objectives   14
  5. Plans of Organization (All courses. See discussion
    under Position 5.)

Jury judgment agreement with the writer's evaluation of this chief guiding element, "The Philosophy as Shown in Statements of the Point of View, Creeds, Aims, Objectives, and Various Plans of Organization" . . . 94 per cent. This agreement was obtained through jury judgment by having experienced persons in the field evaluate the same course of study.

At the outset of this discussion attention is called to the fact that out of meanings, beliefs, and ideals emerging from experience every person has evolved some philosophy of life. This philosophy influences the thinking and the choices of the individual. To be sure, it undergoes change. The thinking of the growing person undergoes continuous change as it grapples with immediate problems pressing for solution or examines the countless presuppositions of inherited thought. The educator cannot escape reflecting his philosophy. The failure to declare a point of view, or even the assertion that none is held, is in itself a reflection of a point of view. "Some philosophy every man has, whether he articulates it or not. A teacher without a guiding philosophy of life is, at best, only an artisan." [45:248] A major problem of the educator, either individually or as a member of a group, is to examine his thinking in the light of the best current opinion in the field. The next step in the same problem is to arrive at a well-balanced guiding philosophy to serve immediate needs and as a vantage point from which to do further critical thinking. Finally, it is most important to the educative process of the child that the guiding philosophy thus attained is consistently put into practice. Of this fundamental element in education Professor Kilpatrick says:

In so far as we have an acceptable philosophy of life, is our school system consistently furthering it? Or does our philosophy point in one way and the features of our school system point varyingly in other directions? What changes should be made in our school system that it may adequately and consistently embody and express the philosophy we accept? . . . consciously or not, adequately or not, each educator placed in any position of responsibility answers in his every act both questions. It is not a problem of whether one shall or shall not have a philosophy of education, but solely and exactly what kind of philosophy one shall have, whether each one of us is to absorb his philosophy unquestioningly by tradition from the prejudices of his chance associates, or whether under competent guidance he is to make a conscious and determined effort to build a philosophy that shall correlate his educational activities with the best that has been thought by man. [40:73]

UNDERLYING ASPECTS ON WHICH THESE FINDINGS
WERE COLLECTED

It should be conducive to a clearer interpretation of the findings on this fundamental aspect of the curriculum problem to clarify briefly the guiding elements here set up. In this case the various aspects used to collect the evidence from printed curricula are stated within the guiding element itself, "The Philosophy as Shown in Statements of the Point of View, Creeds, Aims, Objectives, and Various Plans of Organization."

Out of a background of interesting philosophical thought these guiding elements have emerged as vehicles of expression for the underlying educational philosophy. The concepts which they carry have been modified and changed in response to the many influences which have poured into the body of recent educational thought. Since the beginning of the present century the various aspects upon which this guiding element was set up have traveled far in the change of meanings which they convey. As avenues of expression for the professed philosophy, they appear in most of the current materials in the field. To be sure the philosophy, expressed through these means, may embody the best aspects of current educational thought and yet suggest curriculum situations which trail clouds of traditional procedures and offer many suggestions for unrelated subject matter.

It has been said elsewhere that philosophy seeks to serve education at points where conflict centers. The philosophy of education revealed through the application of this guiding element to the curriculum materials, for the period of this study, shows the outstanding influence of the contribution of John Dewey. It should be noted early in this discussion, as an item of interest to protagonists of this point of view, that there is a marked recognition—in theory, if too often not in practice—of this body of philosophical thought.

It is widely quoted as a source of guidance at the many points of conflict inherent in the curriculum problem. This appears to be true however much the interpretation of this far-reaching contribution may be limited by the curriculum maker's personal philosophy, or by his lack of vision and skill in applying his accepted educational philosophy to the curriculum problem as a whole.

Fundamental to the steadily increasing influence of the philosophy of experimentalism, as voiced by Dewey and others, are its central tenets. Its biological foundation has removed the emphasis from the metaphysical and brought a new concept to the educative process. Its long and consistent stress upon the democratic ideal recognizes a deep-seated national need. Its continual insistence upon an educational program of participation provides practice in democratic daily living. It is a philosophy based solidly upon experience. On this point Professor Childs says:

. . . the ultimate educational aim of experimentalism is to develop individuals who can intelligently manage their own affairs, at times "alone," more usually in shared or joint enterprise. It believes this ideal will be achieved as children are given opportunity to practice it under intelligent guidance in the schools. As the experimentalist conceives it, education is the social process by which human beings are created. [10:93]

In the findings resulting from the use of this guiding element various aspects of Dewey's important contribution to educational thought are frequently stated as his theory, or philosophy, of growth through individual and group experiences. Other theories appear. Various schools of psychology show their influence. Forecasts of tenacious outworn procedures are recorded. From "Statements of the Point of View" through the "Various Plans of Organization" the guiding philosophy of the curriculum maker is revealed.

Discussion of the Findings for "The Philosophy as Shown in State-ments of the Point of View, Creeds, Aims, Objectives, and Various Plans of Organization"

Position 1

Statements of the Point of View . . . 43 per cent (approximately) of the 71 courses examined.

These conditions were found:

	Courses
Total number of courses under Position 1	31
Courses which showed a variety of thought	31

Courses which stated some aspect of the organization of
curriculum materials 6
Courses which emphasized some aspect of subject matter 8
Courses which referred to the "Seven Cardinal Objectives" 3
Courses which used character education 2
Courses which stated some aspect of a theory of edu-
cation as growth 12

This last-mentioned group of courses showed such statements as
"Creative planning by the pupil-teacher group"; "opportunity for
self-expression"; "many everyday experiences," and "use and improvement of the environment."

The courses under position 1 which stated details of the organization as their point of view appeared in the most formal position
under the guiding element dealing with "Subject Matter: How
Thought of and How Accordingly Used." The courses which stated
some aspect of a theory of educational growth as their point of
view appeared in the least formal position under the criterion dealing with subject matter.

The distribution by subjects of the 31 courses in which the guiding philosophy appeared chiefly under this position, "Statements of
the Point of View": general courses—8; social studies—10; art—9;
arithmetic—4.

Position 2

Creeds expressed the guiding philosophy in 11 per cent (approximately) of the 71 courses examined.

These conditions were found:

Courses

Total number of courses under Position 2 8
Courses which stated their philosophy in this form and
showed consistent effort to embody it in the suggested
experiences 8
Courses which appeared in the least formal position set
up for subject matter 8
Courses which stated some aspect of the Dewey philosophy 6
Courses which emphasized the social aspect of experience
both in their guiding philosophy and the suggested experience-situations 5

Distribution by subjects of the 8 courses in which the curriculum
makers' philosophy appeared to a large extent under this position
"Creeds": general courses—2; social studies—6; art—0; arithmetic—0.

Under this position such statements appeared as part of "Our Creed": "We believe that education is living. That living implies growing" [1:iii]. The course which gave this point of view as a part of its guiding philosophy showed a wide variety of rich experience-situations. It reflected utilization and enrichment of the environment and made provision for a wide range of creative experiences. A thorough knowledge of the fundamental laws of child development was steadily apparent. Another course under this position stated: "Activity is not an incidental part of the program. It is the means by which learning takes place." [9:xiiii]

In most of the courses of this group there was a distinct relationship between the professed philosophy and many of the suggested experiences. It seemed as if the form through which this position was frequently expressed, "Our Creed," had placed an added challenge upon the group to carry out what "We believe."

Position 3

Aims expressed the guiding philosophy in 25 per cent (approximately) of the 71 courses examined.

These conditions were found:

	Courses
Total number of courses under Position 3	18
Courses which showed subject matter aims and placed the major emphasis upon acquisition of skills	10
Courses which showed "general aims" for the curriculum as a whole	8
Courses, of the general aims group, which emphasized education as life and applied this point of view to the suggested experiences	4
Courses which appeared in the most formal position set up for subject matter	10
Courses which appeared in the least formal position set up for subject matter	8

Distribution by subjects of the courses in which the curriculum maker's philosophy appeared to a large extent under this position, "Aims": general courses—4; social studies—3; art—3; arithmetic—8.

Under this position, in the group of 4 courses which showed general aims to guide the curriculum experiences and emphasized education as life, such statements as the following appeared as part of the "Aims" of one course: "In its broadest sense education is the organization of all experiences that mold the life of the individual and the community . . . elementary education must give the child those things which will enable him to live fully." [60:19] The same course further expressed its guiding philosophy regarding the child: "He must meet situations in which he experiences the need for subject-matter. He needs to learn it in relation to use." [60:22] The suggested experiences of this course showed a consistent relationship to the curriculum maker's stated point of view.

Any student of the curriculum problem is faced early with the need for careful thought on the question of "Aims." To achieve those which *liberate* rather than *limit* is a continuous and challenging problem. Much emphasis is needed here.

Education is fundamentally an evolving process. It is, moreover, an organic process in the sense that it is cumulatively growing, that it is rooted in the past and is pointing toward the future. Whatever aims we are able to furnish at any stage of that process cannot be considered as final; nor can they be arbitrarily inserted into the subsequent educational process. They are evolving rather than pre-existing. . . . Their value to the educational process lies in their challenging nature, not in their end-state. Development, liberation, the release of energy and thought are the major emphasis of dynamic education and these cannot be achieved by conceiving ends or aims in terms of detailed final outcomes externally introduced. . . . If we attempt to do this, we necessarily limit future possibilities in terms of present actualities. [72:204]

Position 4

Objectives expressed the guiding philosophy in 20 per cent (approximately) of the 71 courses examined.

These conditions were found:

	Courses
Total number of courses under Position 4	14
Courses which showed subject matter objectives	8
Courses which showed "general objectives" for the curriculum as a whole	6
Courses which stated both "general" and "subject matter" objectives and were consistent in applying their point of view to the suggested experiences	2
Courses which emphasized subject matter largely determined in advance, stressed the acquisition of skills, and appeared under the most formal positions set up for the guiding element dealing with subject matter	8
Courses of the "general objectives" group, which appeared in the least formal positions set up for subject matter	6

Distribution by subjects of the 14 courses which expressed their guiding philosophy through "Objectives": general courses—2; social studies—6; art—2; arithmetic—4.

In one of the two courses which showed both general and specific objectives and in which a conscious effort was shown to maintain a well-balanced relationship between the general guiding objectives and those set up for the particular subject in question, these statements appear:

. . . in response to demands of modern life and guided by a new vision of the function of education, the school now opens its doors to a host of experiences and activities which found no place in the classrooms of an earlier day.

Schools should furnish every child an opportunity for work, study, and play. Give him freedom to purpose, to think, to take initiative, to make decisions, and to assume responsibilities. [17:5]

This general point of view is used as the educational climate for such subject matter objectives as, "Children are made aware of the art principles of design, color, texture, and techniques in relation to materials surrounding them and their active use in everyday life situations" [43:6]. These general and specific objectives were followed by many suggested activities to carry out this point of view.

Objectives, serving the curriculum problem in the same general way as Aims, have had much discussion, research, and time centered upon them. Many of the persons concentrating on this field recognize the need of both vision and much careful investigation in order to find guiding lines that will *liberate* rather than *limit* the possible curriculum experiences.

Position 5

Plan of Organization. A brief questionnaire was sent to the superintendent of schools in each of the 35 cities from which the materials for this study were drawn. This was done to check the interpretation of the information recorded in the printed curricula. In a few cases some of the major elements of the organization were not consistently evident and needed to be supplemented. No attempt was made to seek all the elements inherent in the various organizations. Those elements were sought which were considered most outstanding in their influence upon the content and procedures of the educative experiences offered to the child by the elementary school.

In the information recorded from this inquiry there is no claim that some overlapping of the various elements of organization does not exist. However, in all cases where it was reported as predominantly of a certain type it is recorded as such. The response from one city added the information that their organization could not be adequately represented through the inquiry which was made. In fairness to that situation the information given is not included in this record.

The following conditions were found:

Various Plans of Organization which showed:

1. Teacher participation in some aspect of the curriculum problem (as shown in 71 courses and questionnaires from 34 cities)

    Courses

    a. For a small portion of the total group   21
    b. For a fairly large portion of the total group   35
    c. For practically all members of the teaching staff   15

    Cities

2. A program of departmentalized instruction. This was defined as organized upon the basis of subjects and largely taught by separate teachers. (Taken from questionnaire to 34 cities)   14

3. A program of instruction organized with one teacher for each group. This person was largely responsible for all subjects   16

4. A distinctly local type which showed combinations of numbers 2 and 3   5

5. Homogeneous grouping, to some degree, in the so-called regular classes . . . Yes — 19; No — 15

6. An integrated program in which individual differences, except in cases of extreme limitation, were provided for through a wide range of experiences   18

7. Tests in the so-called subject matter field

    Courses

    a. Used through a centrally controlled program to test the acquisition of subject matter and the results made the most determining factor in the promotion of pupils   44

    b. Used solely as an instrument of instruction after recognition by the pupils and teacher jointly as useful to their needs. The results are given only their relative value by the teacher in the total picture of the child's development   27

Some of the Plans of Organization which emphasized a program of highly departmentalized instruction upon the basis of subjects taught by separate teachers also appeared as having an Integrated Program of Experiences. A number of the courses from situations which showed the departmentalized type of organization appeared in the most formal position under the guiding element, "Subject Matter: How Thought of and How Accordingly Used."

The majority of the 44 courses, which showed a centrally controlled testing program used to emphasize the acquisition of subject matter and determine promotion, appeared in the most formal position under subject matter. All of the 27 courses which used tests as an instrument of instruction, recognized by pupils and teacher jointly as useful to their needs, and gave to test results only their relative value in the child's total record, appeared in the least formal position under subject matter.

These findings contribute to the point of view that organization should serve a previously determined educational program rather than have that program limited by unstudied organization. The conditions reflected here call further attention to the wide questioning of homogeneous grouping for results other than the acquisition of so-called formal subject matter. The findings regarding the departmentalized program, organized on the basis of subjects and largely taught by separate teachers, show a condition which forces the instructor to give the subject rather than the child the major consideration. This entails procedures which run counter to the best thought in the field of child development.

The foregoing conditions and other equally contradictory phases in organization are evident. It is easily apparent that the guiding philosophy as it appears in this area, "Various Plans of Organization," reveals confusion. Here is a challenge to our best thinking and investigation for some time to come. The need for thinking through the various aspects at conflict here and squaring procedure with the professed philosophy is vital to the whole curriculum problem. This is a strategic area owing to the fact that many elements converge at this point. Such a condition makes organization one of the chief means through which the educational philosophy in use is revealed and a main avenue for the functioning of other elements fundamental to rich curriculum experiences.

It is apparent that much of our present organization was inherited without question. Certain phases have grown up without direction. More recent innovations have not always squared their procedures with their own stated point of view. Much wholesale copying of types of organization has taken place without sufficient consideration of the underlying principles or their appropriateness to the immediate situation. Provision for study and acceptance of a particular type of organization by the teaching staff as a whole has not always been made. This runs counter to fundamental democratic procedure that all persons affected should participate in a decision. Regarding this question of participation Newlon writes:

> The classroom teacher must share in the task of outlining an educational policy for the country which will accord with our noblest concepts of the high civilization that may be achieved in the United States. [53:xiii]

Certain aspects of organizations linger after the conditions have passed which they were supposed to serve. Some situations show that their organization blocks rather than promotes the most constructive elements in their educational program. Some courses which stated a guiding philosophy for their curriculum program showed that it had not been applied to the organization. A co-operatively determined, but tentative, guiding philosophy' should shape the educational program. This same guiding philosophy applied to organization should cause it to *serve* rather than *limit* this program. Newlon, an outstanding authority in the field of administration, says:

> The educative process . . . is conditioned by the character of the control and administration of the school. . . . The best recommendations may be entirely frustrated by administrative practices that are at variance with principles on which the recommendations are based or that fail to provide the conditions necessary for carrying them into effect. [53:xiii]

It is reasonable to believe that there will be increasingly rich learning experiences provided for growing children as this social point of view permeates administration, and more persons having continuous first-hand contacts with the educational program have a voice in shaping the conditions affecting this program. Such a provision will release and capitalize contributions which should have their influence all along the line—from more dynamic experience-situations in the curriculum to more educative buildings and equipment.

It would, then, seem distinctly unwise for the best interests of all concerned that organization should ever be considered apart from the total educational program which it serves. Variety in organization there must always be. This is vital to growth and fundamental to the critical thinking inherent in progress.

Whether the professed philosophy of the curriculum makers appears in "Statements of the Point of View, Creeds, Aims, Objectives, or Various Plans of Organization," it is important that it should undergo continuous examination in the light of the best current opinion in the field. This is necessary in order that the philosophy of education may serve the curriculum problem at points where conflict of opinion centers and in the process of serving, be further developed. According to Childs,

> It is the business of a philosophy of education to make clear what is involved in the action which is carried on within the educational field. . . . We believe that it will be helpful if those who disagree in practice, in the courses of action they are following, will also clarify and expose the grounds for their policies: in short, develop and formulate *their* philosophies of education. [23:288]

SUMMARY

The findings under teacher participation reflect the loss of possible contributions which should be vital to the curriculum problem because of the direct contact with children. Departmentalized instruction and homogeneous grouping continue in spite of much current opinion regarding their negative influence upon the well-rounded development of the growing child. The findings under number 7 for "Plans of Organization, page 37," show that the use of tests is a problem needing much attention. There is evidence that the professed philosophy should be applied to the organization to assist in correcting the confusion which is apparent in that area. This is necessary in order that organization serve the educational program rather than limit it. Departmentalized instruction forces the emphasis to be placed upon subject matter rather than upon the child.

Positions 3 and 4, "Aims" and "Objectives," showed more concern for "subject matter." Positions 1 and 2, "Statements of the

Point of View" and "Creeds," were more sensitive to the total problem, and appeared in the courses estimated in the most informal positions set up for subject matter. The courses in these groups showed more relationship between the professed philosophy and the suggested experiences.

II. BUILDING THE PERSONALITY AS A WHOLE

As Characterized in the "Guide for the Evaluation of Elementary Curricula" and Found Through Its Use

Does this course provide for experiences planned toward the positive up-building of the personality of the child through:

A. Provision for a wholesome continuous program of rich and varied individual and group experience-situations which has been planned toward building the personality in all its varied bearings and aspects.

B. Provision in the suggested program for experiences which embody conservation of and growth in physical well-being, through the development of recreational habits and appreciations, as a foundation for well-balanced emotional and mental development.

C. Provision for socialized self-activity, realized through: participation; freedom, with respect for the needs and rights of the group, to explore and manipulate; self-help; creativity.

D. Provision for the orientation of self to the social surroundings through: communication; friendliness; sharing; co-operation; respect for the personalities and rights of others.

E. Provision for choice and decision regarding experience-situations which have vital significance to the child; increasing use of the best out-of-school experiences; choice and effective use of materials necessary to carry through the chosen undertaking to a satisfactory solution; sharing, evaluating, and enjoying the results.

F. Provision for the recognition by the pupil and teacher of the need of useful habits and essential skills, appropriate to that level of development, and provision for acquiring them; opportunities to build an attitude of individual and group approval toward the courage and clear thinking necessary for intelligent objection.

G. Provision for the continuous utilization of opportunities for further integrated growth as they arise in the program of suggested experience-situations planned toward the positive upbuilding of the personality as a whole.

Positions which this course may reflect under the guiding element, "Building the Personality as a Whole":

1. Little or no suggestion of experiences which have been planned to provide opportunities for building the personality as a whole.

2. Some provision inherent in the suggested experiences, but little emphasis given to opportunities for building the personality.

3. Definite provision for many experience-situations which offer rich opportunities for building the personality as a whole.

Positions, as defined above, found for this fundamental guiding element through the examination of 71 courses of study:

Position	Number of Courses
1	6
2	37
3	28

Jury judgment agreement with the writer's evaluation of the provision for "Building the Personality as a Whole" . . . 96 per cent.

It is pertinent to the interpretation of the findings that the concept herein used for "personality" be clarified early in the discussion. It is intended that the term should carry a depth and inclusiveness of meaning which is not always implied when it refers to surface appearances, largely determined upon short time exposure, or when, in cases of negative conclusions, it is too frequently tied up with difference of opinion on some problem under discussion. Personality, as the concept is here used, is based upon and reflects the self in its long process of development—its up-building, as a whole. As Mead points out,

The self has a character which is different from that of the physiological organism proper. The self is something which has a development: it is not initially there, at birth, but arises in the process of social experience and activity, that is, develops in the given individual as a result of his relations to that process as a whole and to other individuals within that process. [44:135]

On the up-building of the self Professor Kilpatrick says:

To up-build the self is then to improve one's working stock of meanings, making them ever more numerous, ever more inclusive of the rich potentialities of life, ever better validated, better and better refined and defined, ever better organized—and finally ever better and better obeyed as these better meanings are efficiently worked up into appropriate plans of action. [39:12]

While the self is thus being built out of what is learned through these new meanings, it is also being related to the life in which it exists. The degree of personal integration of the new meanings is important. The quality of the structure of the self is reflected in the personality.

The foregoing concept of personality implies the possibility of growth throughout life. In the process of developing the self as the foundation of building the personality, this concept implies the pre-existence of the group, inter-action of individuals within the group, certain co-operative activities, and the total reaction of the individual to his total environment. Building the personality becomes a two-way process. Here, we have reflected the individual in his reaction to his environment and to his inner self.

The study of the human personality involves the attempt to penetrate beneath surface appearance and conventional expressions to the dynamic factors of human nature, to reach the real individual beneath. . . . The term personality has a certain social reference; it signifies the individual in his reaction to his environment as well as in his inner experience. [8:2]

The inclusiveness of this concept gives to the building of the personality the importance which it should receive. It presents a challenge to the school to provide a rich and varied learning environment for the child. This is fundamental to increasing the store of meanings necessary to the up-building of the self as the foundation for "Building the Personality as a Whole."

UNDERLYING ASPECTS ON WHICH THESE FINDINGS WERE COLLECTED

It may assist the reader to a better understanding of the discussion of this vital phase of the curriculum experiences to further define this guiding element as set up. The aspects mentioned at the beginning of this section were incorporated in the guide used for evaluating printed curricula regarding its provision for "Building the Personality as a Whole."

The importance of a program of experience-situations which are rich and varied stands out. Learning through experiencing, including many situations to be solved which are vital to the child, is held fundamental to growth. The wide range of interests is to be served through variety in the experiences made possible. The school is to reflect the most constructive elements in life situations and provide continuous practice in individual and group relationships. Such a program is considered fundamental to increasing—as well as enriching—the store of meanings of which the self is built. The marked advance in the attitude and techniques for health conservation and emotional adjustment is recognized as making a vital contribution. The self is socialized through continuous participation with the group and by means of many relationships with the environment. This is done in much the same way as the self is slowly built up through what is learned.

Among further aspects set up under this guiding element is that of pupil-teacher participation in the selection of experiences vital to the group. It follows that carrying out the chosen undertaking, sharing its challenges and difficulties, recognizing and acquiring needed skills, evaluating and enjoying the results are all made contributing factors in the total experience. The opportunity to build an attitude of approval toward the courage and clear thinking necessary for intelligent objection is given its rightful place. Not only are these experiences offered and held basic to the end in view but their utilization to this end is consistently advocated. Such a program is conceived as making a contribution toward building the personality in its varied bearings and aspects.

DISCUSSION OF THE FINDINGS FOR
"BUILDING THE PERSONALITY AS A WHOLE"

Position 1

Little or no suggestion of experiences which have been planned to provide opportunities for building the personality as a whole . . . 8 per cent (approximately) of the 71 courses which were examined.

These conditions were found:

	Courses
Total number of courses under Position 1	6
Courses which showed little or no provision for experiences planned toward building the personality	6
Courses which stated subject matter objectives as their professed philosophy	6
Courses which stated a guiding point of view for the curriculum as a whole	0
Courses which appeared in the most formal position set up for subject matter	5
Courses which appeared in a somewhat less formal position under subject matter	1

The distribution by subjects of the 6 courses of this group which made little or no provision for, "Building the Personality as a Whole": general courses—2; social studies—o; art—o; arithmetic—4. The courses of this group were among those which were evaluated as showing no recognition of or provision for creative experience. There is little evidence of the type of experience which gives promise of the positive up-building of the personality.

Position 2

Some provision inherent in the suggested experiences, but little emphasis given to opportunities for building the personality . . . 52 per cent (approximately.) of the 71 courses examined.

These conditions were found:

	Courses
Total number of courses under Position 2	37
Courses which showed a guiding point of view for the curriculum as a whole as well as subject matter objectives	12
Courses, of the group just mentioned, which were fairly consistent in carrying over their professed philosophy into their suggested experiences	7
Courses, of the group of 7, which used character education as their general aim	2
Courses which showed subject matter aims and made no statement of a guiding point of view for the curriculum as a whole	23
Courses which were listed under the two most formal positions set up for subject matter	23
Courses, of the group of 23, which had 5 to 15 per cent of their materials estimated in the least formal position set up for subject matter	8

Courses which showed both general and subject matter objectives and had the major portion of their materials estimated in the least formal positions under subject matter   12
Courses which showed the most consistency between the professed philosophy and the suggested educational experiences   12

Distribution by subjects of the 37 courses which showed some provision inherent in their materials, but gave little emphasis to opportunities for building the personality as a whole: general courses—5; social studies—7; art—1; arithmetic—14. These courses, as a group, showed some experiences which could have been used for the positive up-building of the personality but little emphasis was given to this aspect of the educative process.

The findings under this position, "Building the Personality as a Whole," stand out as especially challenging. That any opportunity to contribute to this major aspect of the educative process is not fully capitalized by its recognition and use should carry valuable implications to guide future curriculum efforts.

Position 3

Definite provision for many wholesome experience-situations which offer rich opportunities for building the personality . . . 39 per cent (approximately) of the 71 courses examined.

These conditions were found:

	Courses
Total number of courses under Position 3	28
Courses which stated a guiding point of view for the curriculum as a whole and subject matter objectives	25
Courses, of the group just mentioned, which showed consistency in carrying over their professed philosophy into their suggested experiences	15
Courses which had the major portion of their materials estimated in the least formal position under subject matter	25

This group of courses showed frequent mention in their professed philosophy of the need for developing the individual as a whole and offered a wide variety of suggested experiences: Distribution by subjects of the 28 courses which showed provision for experience-situations offering opportunities for building the personality as a whole: general courses—8; social studies—16; art—4; arithmetic—0.

As the evaluation of the curriculum materials of these courses showed so-called subject matter moving toward the least formal positions, an increase in the number of social studies courses appeared. The courses of this group showed the most consistent relationship between their professed philosophy and the suggested educational experiences. They revealed also the most provision for rich and varied experience-situations which are fundamental to increasing the store of meanings as the self is built up through what is learned.

The following excerpts from the courses of this group reflect the point of view on this fundamental aspect of the educative process and show the curriculum maker's attempt to provide many elements toward building the personality. From a course which has suggested many experience-situations, this statement stands out:

Facts are raw material and cannot be scorned. As essential as they are, they are not valuable until tied together and translated into ideas. They should not be given to the student by the teacher, but experiences of the unit should make it possible for the student to arrive at these or similar generalizations. [26:24]

From another course which showed a rich program of suggested experiences and recognized the need for checking up on resulting habits and attitudes is this important statement: "Many children showed increasing ability to stay with their self-chosen tasks and to set higher standards for their work." [14:iii] Another course points out: "Probably the use of books should be regarded as a supplement to first-hand experiences rather than as the main type of activity." [16:140] This much needed suggestion is taken from a course which is outstanding in its provision for rich and varied experience-situations: "He finds in the teacher one who listens to the tale of his experiences and his natural desire to do. She will encourage questioning." [67:280] A course, which reflected its evaluation of outcomes, largely by means of the teacher's judgment of growth, considered this important element necessary to child development: "Shows increasing pleasure in participating in group activities." [35:43]

It has been stated that the concept of personality used for this discussion implies growth throughout life. The elementary schools' contribution to this long and complex development occurs during crucial years. A continuous program of rich and varied experience-situations to increase the store of meanings and their applications should be made available to all children. Many situations to be met, which are vital to the child, should be provided to afford continuous opportunities for the integration of the self. Out of such provision the self is built and, according to Wheeler and Perkins: "The personality evolves, a single pattern of behavior, with each act depending upon every other *while it is emerging.*" [76:472]

SUMMARY

The findings under positions 1 and 2 show that 60 per cent of the materials examined made no conscious provision for building the personality as a whole. This fact may well challenge the attention of all persons who recognize in this guiding element an inclusive end point of education. The findings under position 3 show that 39 per cent of the materials made definite provision for experiences which gave promise of contributing to this end—a fact which should verify that some progress has been made.

The concept which is used for personality in this discussion is intended to carry a depth and inclusiveness of meaning which is not usually implied by the term. The curriculum maker's concept of personality was largely synonymous with his point of view on the curriculum as a whole. Personality, as here used, is based upon and reflects the self in its long process of up-building. The school is challenged to present a rich and varied learning environment based upon experiences vital to the child. This is fundamental to increasing his store of meanings and necessary to the up-building of the self. Building the personality becomes a two-way process. Here we have reflected the individual in his reaction to his environment and to his inner self. The courses which made definite provision for the various aspects set up under this inclusive guiding element showed more relationship between the professed philosophy and their suggested educational experiences.

III. THE PLACE OF ENVIRONMENT IN LEARNING

As Characterized in the "Guide for the Evaluation of Elementary Curricula" and Found through Its Use

Does this course recognize the importance of the actual environment in learning by providing for the use of:

A. *The natural environment.* Physical features; phases of animal and plant life; interesting geological formations; physical forces of the environment; other natural elements of interest in that locality.

B. *The social environment.* Relationship to the various groups: the home; the school; play and club experiences; community—national and international groups.

C. *The esthetic environment.* Beauty of form and color in the things of daily life: arts and crafts products; beauty in nature; architecture; masterpieces of art, in all forms of expression.

Positions which this course may reflect on "The Place of Environment in Learning."

1. No mention of the conscious utilization of the environment.
2. Utilization of the environment *as found*.
3. Enrichment and utilization of the environment.
4. A combination of positions. This combination was suggested where the examiner thought it would yield a fairer reaction to the materials being examined.

Positions, as defined above, found for "The Place of Environment in Learning" through the examination of 71 courses of study:

Position	Number of Courses
1	6
2	12
3	0
4 (a combination of 2 and 3)	53

Jury judgment agreement with the writer's evaluation of curriculum materials through the use of this guiding element . . . 89 per cent (approximately).

Fundamental to the point of view underlying this discussion is the conception of the environment as the other pole from the individual in the learning situation. All living creatures exist in some type of environment. On their adjustment to or mastery of its elements depends their existence. The human organism makes countless reactions to its surroundings during a lifetime. These reactions to new aspects in the immediate environment, to the solution of which the organism brings its past experience in meeting new situations, may be termed learning. The inter-relation of the learner and the environment is so bound up that one does not exist in the learning situation without the other. This inter-action goes on to some degree continually. The individual is exposed to it throughout his life. Whatever aspect of the total environment may predominate —the natural, the social, the esthetic—or whether that aspect exists to a rich or impoverished degree, the learner is at the other end of the environment receiving-set and is continually sensitive to its messages. On this point Dewey says: ". . . the educative process which goes on willy-nilly is to lead us to note that the only way in which adults consciously control the kind of education which the immature get is by controlling the environment in which they act, and hence think and feel." [20:22]

With the environment in the learning situation defined as the other pole from the learner and with the inclusive definition of environment set up under this criterion, the concept here used of learning, itself, must of necessity be an inclusive one. It is intended to avoid the too frequently narrow interpretation and consider learning for what it is—a process affecting the human organism in its total experience. "Learning has ceased to be regarded as a simple process of assimilation of materials and memorization, and has come to be viewed as a process affecting the human organism in the totality of its activity and experiences." [72:147]

UNDERLYING ASPECTS ON WHICH THESE FINDINGS WERE COLLECTED

Some definition of the aspects and positions under the guiding element, "The Place of Environment in Learning," should assist in a clearer interpretation of the findings.

In recognizing the three aspects—the natural, the social, and the esthetic—as outstanding in the total environment, it was not intended that either one should be used to the exclusion of the others in a particular learning situation. It is frequently true, however, that one aspect may predominate while others are present. Rich experience-situations draw widely upon many fields and use all aspects of this guiding element.

Every individual finds himself in a natural environment. Ways of responding to the outstanding physical features and forces of his surroundings have come to him as part of the race inheritance. As he gradually explores his natural environment, its various elements take on new meanings. The plant and animal life, the geological formations, and other interesting natural features present a continuing challenge for investigation. If his guidance has been wise, the foundation for a life interest in the world of nature is frequently laid. The fields of science and exploration constantly pour new discoveries into the present interesting body of knowledge. This new knowledge in turn presents new ways of responding to the environment.

The social environment surrounds and influences the learner in many ways too subtle to analyze. The home, the school, the play and other group influences, the community, the national and international groups all make their contribution in varying ways and to varying degrees. It would be difficult to imagine an environment in which the social aspect did not function largely. Taba writes:

. . . organized race experience, through all its forms of expression (books, ideas, related facts, institutions, generalized concepts, established forms of social living and thinking), provides means for widening the scope of direct experience, which if limited to the possibilities of immediate contacts with the living environment would of necessity be incomplete. However, an equally important source for learning is provided by contact with the living environment of today, both social and physical. The conduct of learners is greatly affected by their contacts with the immediate environment. Facts, ideas, opinions are acquired in the process of direct living. Patterns of conduct are determined by surrounding conditions. The individual's character is moulded through communication with other people. [72:220]

The importance of the esthetic environment in daily life is receiving increasing recognition. Beauty of form and color in the products of the industrial world are becoming more apparent. The arts and crafts products, beauty in nature, architecture, and masterpieces of art in all forms of expression enrich the environment for the use of the learner. Of the esthetic in daily life Bonser says:

I believe:

That the materials of industry—paper and woods and metals and clay and fibers—must be regarded as but media for the expression of life problems with beauty of form and color as inseparable elements in its resolution.

That the mission of art is to teach a love of beautiful clothes, beautiful households, beautiful utensils, beautiful surroundings, and all to the end that life itself may be rich and full of beauty in its harmony, its purposes, and its ideals.

That the appreciation of beauty in the thousand common things of daily life will result in the final appreciation of beauty as a dissociated ideal.

That children have the inalienable right to the inspiration and uplift of those rare spirits whose creative genius has given us the masterpieces of art in all its forms. [5:xv]

Most educators recognize the inter-relationship between the learner and his environment as a determining factor in the educative process. Provision for the full range in points of view has been made through the various positions set up under this guiding element, "The Place of Environment in Learning." Under position 1, the lack of the conscious utilization of this element would not eliminate some measure of its influence, although it is maintained that the experience-situations of the curriculum under this position reflect less richness. Under position 2, utilization of the environment, as found, should be a practical means of capitalizing usable elements, revealing its limitations, and creating the desire to improve it. Under position 3, the term "enrichment" carries the concept of the schools' responsibility to eliminate, simplify, and balance the environment to the needs of the growing child.

DISCUSSION OF THE FINDINGS FOR
"THE PLACE OF ENVIRONMENT IN LEARNING"

Position 1

No mention of the conscious utilization of the environment . . . 8 per cent (approximately) of the 71 courses examined.

These conditions were found:

	Courses
Total number of courses under Position 1	6
Courses which showed no mention of the conscious utilization of the environment either in the professed philosophy or the suggested experiences	6
Courses which showed a guiding philosophy applied to the problem as a whole	0

Courses which stated subject matter objectives under the guiding element dealing with the philosophy	5
Courses which stated a general objective but showed little evidence of its application to the problem as a whole	1
Courses which appeared under the most formal position set up for subject matter	5

Distribution by subjects of the 6 courses of this group, which made no mention of the conscious utilization of the environment: general courses—2; social studies—1; art—0; arithmetic—3. There was little or no evidence under this position of any relationship between a professed philosophy and the suggested educational experiences.

Position 2

Utilization of the environment, as found . . . 16 per cent (approximately) of the 71 courses examined.

These conditions were found:

	Courses
Total number of courses under Position 2	12
Courses which showed some recognition of the use of the environment, as found, either in the professed philosophy or in the suggested experiences	12
Courses which showed the use of the environment both in the professed philosophy and the suggested experiences	4
Courses which appeared under the most formal position set up for subject matter	5
Courses which appeared under the less formal positions set up for subject matter	7
Courses which stated a point of view to guide the problem as a whole and appeared under the most informal position set up for subject matter	3

Distribution by subjects of the 12 courses which utilized the environment, as found: general courses—1; social studies—0; art—0; arithmetic—11.

It is interesting to note that all the courses of this group except 1 were in the field of arithmetic. The utilization of the environment, *as found*, in the field of number experiences should lead the way toward the more inclusive concept of the enrichment of number experiences. Such a tendency to eliminate, simplify, and balance the number experiences would have a far-reaching influence in making the contribution from this field increasingly dynamic.

Position 3

Enrichment and utilization of the environment

No courses appeared wholly under position 3. This was due to the suggestion that a combination of positions might be used in cases in which the examiner thought this procedure would lend itself to a fairer reaction to the materials under consideration.

Position 4

A combination of positions 2 and 3 . . . 76 per cent (approximately) of the 71 courses examined. Accompanying the suggestion to use a combination of positions, the request was made for an estimate of the per cent of the material which appeared under each position used.

These conditions were found:

	Courses
Total number of courses under the Combination Position 2 and 3	53
A. Findings having larger per cent under Position 2	
Courses which had 50 to 85 per cent of their materials estimated under Position 2	25
Courses which had 15 to 50 per cent of their materials estimated under Position 3	25
Courses of this group of 25 which recognized the importance of the environment in their professed philosophy and showed some application of it to their suggested experiences	14
Courses of this group of 25 which appeared in the two most formal positions set up for subject matter	11
Courses of this group of 25 which appeared under the least formal position	9
Courses of this group of 25 which expressed some aspect of education as growth as their professed philosophy	16
Courses of this group of 25 which stated their point of view for this position and were consistent in carrying it out	8

Distribution by subjects of the courses in this group: general courses —8; social studies—7; art—7; arithmetic—3.

B. Findings having larger per cent under Position 3	
Courses within the combination Position 2 and 3 which had 50 to 90 per cent of their materials estimated under Position 3	28
Courses which had 10 to 50 per cent of their materials estimated under Position 2	28
Courses of this group of 28 which recognized the impor-	

tance of enriching and using the environment in their professed philosophy and made some provision for it in their suggested experiences 19

Courses which appeared under the least formal position set up for subject matter 15

Courses which appeared under the two most formal positions 6

Courses which showed some aspect of the theory of education as growth 17

Courses which stated a point of view on this position of the environment and were consistent in applying it to their suggested experiences 9

Distribution by subjects of the 28 courses in this group: general courses—5; social studies—14; art—8; arithmetic—1.

As the point of view moved over from a right to a left position and as the suggested experience-situations increased in apparent richness, the number of social studies and art courses increased in the group. On the whole, Group A of this combination position 2 and 3 showed a much wider use of the environment than the preceding situation defined solely as position 2. Group B under the same combination position showed a richer use of the environment than Group A. In guiding point of view, quality of suggested experiences, and consistency in the inter-relationship between these two elements, this group was the most outstanding under the guiding element, "The Place of Environment in Learning."

This element in the learning situation has been previously defined as the other pole from the learner. "Not only is the whole organism thus involved in the learning experience, the environment also is involved." [39:8] Because of the degree of importance that environment holds in the educative process the necessity for its wisest possible use grows apace with the increasing interest in the curriculum as a whole.

Further evidence is given of the importance of the environment, as presented in recent courses of study:

It is important that the teacher understand the part of the environment in the education of the child. It not only furnishes the stimulus, but from it the child learns many things. It helps to build his ideas. His language is the result of his environment, as are his customs, his standards of right and wrong, his appreciations, his habits of clothing, diet, sleeping, bathing, recreation, religious observance, and the kind of reading he likes. [60:47]

This point of view is embodied in a rich program of suggested experience-situations.

In another course this thought was recorded: "We have taken into account the child's environment." [13:8] The suggested experiences of this course showed that they had been based upon the information thus gained. According to Dewey:

> The first office of the social organ we call the school is to provide a simplified environment . . ., to eliminate, so far as possible, the unworthy features of the existing environment . . ., to balance the various elements in the social environment, and see to it that each individual gets an opportunity . . . to come into living contact with a broader environment. [20:24]

SUMMARY

The findings under this guiding element showed an awareness of the environment and some type of use made of it in the major portion of the materials examined. Under this guiding element the environment in the learning situation is defined as the other pole from the learner. This implies a broader concept of learning and deals with it for what it is—a process affecting the total organism. A well-balanced environment embodying many challenging experience-situations for the child is fundamental to the curriculum problem. The courses which made the most definite provision for this type of program showed the most consistent application of their professed philosophy to the suggested educational experiences.

IV. THE CURRICULUM MAKER'S THEORY OF THE WAY LEARNING TAKES PLACE

As Characterized in the "Guide for the Evaluation of Elementary Curricula" and Found through Its Use

What position does this course show regarding the way learning takes place?

A. *Learning as training.* This position considers learning as training the mind and developing the powers of its faculties.

B. *Learning as the development of ideas through the assimilation of information.* In this position the mastery of information is stressed. Intellectual learning receives the major emphasis. Little attention is given to the social, emotional, and other learnings.

C. *Learning as a process affecting the human organism in its total experience.* In this position learning is a continuing process of enrichment of meanings and accompanying aspects. It involves a situation, a choice of means to meet the situation, and a change in the learner as the situation is met. This change means a cross section of all the aspects of the learner's experience and gives to its social, emotional, and other aspects equal emphasis with the intellectual.

Positions which this course may reflect on "The Curriculum Maker's Theory of the Way Learning Takes Place":

1. Learning as training.
2. Learning as the development of ideas through the assimilation of information.
3. Learning as a process affecting the human organism in its total experience.
4. A combination of any of the above positions.

The use of a combination of positions was suggested in cases where the examiner thought this procedure would yield a fairer reaction to the materials under consideration.

Positions, as defined above, found for "The Curriculum Maker's Theory of the Way Learning Takes Place" through the examination of 71 courses of study:

Position	Number of Courses
1	3
2	8
3	35
4 (A combination of any of the above positions)	25

Jury judgment agreement with the writer's evaluation of curriculum materials through the use of this guiding element . . . 96 per cent (approximately).

The way learning takes place in the educative process is fundamental to the curriculum problem—so much so that all persons co-operating in serious undertakings in this field should make an attempt at the outset to clarify their thinking in the light of the best psychological opinion and declare some point of view to guide their work. This point of view should be a temporary one, to be sure, and subject to further critical thinking in the light of new findings. Any avoidance of this basic need—the best possible point of view on the way learning takes place—carries possibilities of reducing the effectiveness of the curriculum suggestions and contributing to further confusion. That some of our curriculum thinking has been done without meeting this issue squarely is apparent. Its importance as an underlying determining factor throughout all curriculum change is recognized by those persons dealing with the problem as a whole. Whether the way learning takes place is considered early or late in the procedure used for meeting the curriculum problem, we cannot escape reckoning with this fundamental element. The various points of view on this issue and their resulting procedures have appeared in and throughout the ferment of thought on the problem. This has been conspicuously apparent since the turn of the present century and during the last decade of the preceding one. ". . . the content of the curriculum, the methods of teaching, and the specific ways of conducting the educative process, are all directed by the views held on the nature of learning." [72:147] The thinking recorded on this aspect of the educative process has been closely associated with the findings in the field of psychology and the guidance offered by the best contributions of philosophy to current educational thought.

UNDERLYING ASPECTS ON WHICH THESE FINDINGS WERE COLLECTED

It seems pertinent to a clearer interpretation of the findings on this influential aspect of the curriculum problem to discuss briefly the major elements underlying the various positions of this guiding element, "The Curriculum Maker's Theory of the Way Learning Takes Place."

Although the psychology of learning has passed through drastic changes in recent educational movements there still exists traces of the influence of outworn ideas and positions. This condition is reflected throughout much of the current curriculum material. The educational practices frequently suggested show a confusion of conflicting trends. That this condition is true might well be expected as the result of several influences: first, the rapidity with which the new experimental psychology of the present century has poured its findings into the stream of educational thought; second, the persistent tendency in education for practice to lag far behind the theory accepted to guide the program as a whole; third, the too frequent lack of a specific attempt to square procedures with the point of view used for specific elements or for the entire problem.

The changes through which the psychology of learning has passed and the high points of the influences producing these' changes are both interesting and relevant to the current points of view. The new century inherited from the last decades of the old a thriving tendency for psychology to declare its independence from its long and close association with philosophy. This movement was the outgrowth of several influences reaching back into the nineteenth century. Chief among these influences were the two newly developed sciences of chemistry and physiology. Of the former Woodworth says: "The wonderful achievements of chemistry led to the idea of a 'mental chemistry' which should analyze mental compounds into their elements." [77:7] It was during this period that the idea of an analytical psychology, following the procedures of chemistry for the mental sphere, became well established. The influence of the other new science, physiology, was more far-reaching than that of chemistry. The problems of psychology were more closely allied to physiology than to chemistry. As physiology turned to effective experimentation it opened the way for psychology to follow, so that the psychological laboratory was the natural outgrowth of its physiological predecessor. The new experimental psychology came out of the laboratories. It began to make itself felt early in the new century. The protagonists of this movement insisted that evidence must be drawn from definite recorded observations.

Among other influences contributing to the psychological scene of this period was that drawn from the field of biology, especially the theory of evolution. Anthropology made its contribution. The influence of heredity and environment on the mental development of the individual and the race was widely discussed. The work of Darwin and Galton was outstanding. Tests for measuring individuals were devised for use in making this type of study. Developments in the field of psychiatry had been very rapid during the nineteenth century. All these influences had opened up investigations and developed techniques which lent their weight toward divorcing psychology from its long relationship to philosophy and grouping it with the natural sciences. According to Woodworth:

In theory, they [the psychologists of 1900] were for an analytical psychology patterned after chemistry; . . . in practice they often disregarded this scheme. . . . In theory they were strong for a physiological psychology, but in practice they made a profound bow to the brain and passed on their way. [77:12]

The small but aggressive group of experimental psychologists hoped to explore new fields, develop new techniques, and recruit new members. From such a psychological situation the contemporary psychologies have been developed. Out of the ferment of thought centering around the various schools progress has been made. The thinking of each group has contributed its body of influence toward building the present whole. The old faculty psychology based on its metaphysical assumptions, the associationists largely represented in this country through the Herbartian movement, and the steady growth of the newer biological psychology have formed the main influences in this field since the last decades of the preceding century.

The experimental emphasis of the new biological psychology has had a far-reaching influence. This recent school has in turn developed various groups. The behaviorists, the psychoanalysts, the purposivists, and the followers of Gestalt all have contributed from their particular points of view to the contemporary psychological thought as a whole and to the theory of how learning takes place. Authorities in the field say that some schools of thought have stressed making psychology more scientific, while others have emphasized making it more human and adequate. With these two tendencies inherent in contemporary thought, it should be the aim of all persons interested in education to encourage the development of both.

Out of such a background, the way learning takes place has been and is increasingly important in all the points of view. The swing of the pendulum from a highly analytical concept of learning to that of learning as a process affecting the human organism in its total experience is in progress.

For the purpose of applying this guiding element three positions have been set up. The traditional idea of learning, as supported by faculty psychology, considered all learning as training of the mind and developing the powers of its faculties. While few educators of today would accept this point of view, there is evidence of its use in the evaluation of curriculum materials, and the procedures of teaching developed under it are still practiced. Training the mind is still a deeply ingrained idea. In many cases both subjects and devices suggested in curriculum materials are there for their reputed value in this line. On this problem Taba writes: ". . . the tenacity of our schools in catering to the so-called higher. faculties, under-emphasizing other aspects of personality, clearly shows that the effects of the faculty theory of learning are still active." [72:148] Position 1, learning as training, under the guiding element, "The Curriculum Maker's Theory of the Way Learning Takes Place," has been set up to collect the findings on this traditional point of view.

The view of learning as the development of ideas through the assimilation of information is still very common. This is the basis of the Herbartian apperception theory. Many evaluations of curriculum materials are made on the evidence of information and knowledge as an educational standard. This point of view stresses the intellectual. It gives less attention to the social, emotional, and other aspects of learning. Taba emphasizes this condition as follows:

Mastery of information and knowledge is an educational standard, in terms of which many evaluations are effected. The intellectualistic dualism implied by such views on learning is present very strongly in the most progressive educational practices, as is clearly seen in the dispute over the psychological and the logical organization of learning materials, and in the preference for the intellectual subjects over the so-called vocational ones in so far as their educative value is concerned. Learning still too often means intellectual learning only, and as such is regarded as different from the changes brought about in man's behaviour by his ordinary experience. [72:148]

While there exists some evidence of a promising trend to consider curriculum experiences for their social values—their worth to actual behavior and life—education is largely conducted in terms of information and knowledge. Position 2, learning as the development of ideas through the assimilation of information, has been set up to collect the findings on this point of view.

It has been mentioned elsewhere that the science of chemistry had a marked influence in building up the idea of an analytical psychology. This influence was especially strong during the latter part of the nineteenth century and its influence carried over into the early years of the twentieth. It affected both content and procedures.

Into such a setting the new biological psychology based upon experimentation was introduced. There were a number of misleading concepts regarding learning. One of the most outstanding has been the concept that information and knowledge were made educative when organized and graded on the basis of their complexity and the learner's apperceptive ability. Out of this conviction a large body of abstract knowledge came to be accepted as fundamental. Organization and practices have been developed to teach this body of knowledge efficiently. The educational values set upon it have become cemented into the curriculum thought. Its influence grips many of the attempts to seek release from the stereotyped patterns of formal education. Curriculum materials show activities and projects selected and evaluated in terms of school subjects or some long accepted cultural field. When learning is considered as training the mind or when understood as the development of ideas through the assimilation of information and knowledge, it implies that the mind is an entity functioning independently of the rest of the behavior of the individual. With respect to this segregation, Taba says:

Human experience is thus artificially split up, its functions arbitrarily divided and segregated. The result is that anything ensuing from learning conducted in such terms is not integrated in the actual behaviour, and is therefore useless stock. The functions of the mind, when treated and cultivated in separation from the organic unity that is productive of them, namely, the total behaviour, naturally do not offer themselves to the service of this behaviour. And materials assimilated outside the demands of actual behaviour remain inert and unproductive of improvement in conduct. [72:149]

Until behaviorism began to influence the situation, most educational programs recorded since 1900 show that more thought has been concentrated upon the materials of instruction than upon the effect they might have upon the learner's behavior. The learner himself was conspicuously out of the picture. His role was that of a passive recipient. His job was to assimilate the abstract materials of instruction apportioned out according to the grade patterns fixed in advance by those in control of education. The learner did not enter as an active factor into the choice of materials, the determination of procedures, or the evaluation of outcomes. In short, the materials of instruction received more consideration than the learner. For the behaviorist "human behavior has come to mean all observable behavior, and learning the modification and re-modification of that behavior in all its aspects." [72:151] This point of view on learning placed the materials of instruction in a subordinate position to the learner. These were two of the important contributions of behaviorism—learning as behavior and the subordination of the materials of instruction. However, the movement carried its defects. It employed the method of the exact sciences and used the type of learning situations which would yield to this procedure. While it freed learning from the domination of subject matter, it made it dependent upon external stimulation. Learning was considered as behavior and a way to modify it was presented. The human organism was considered as a self-determining unit but the activity involved took on the nature of passive response to the pressure of fixed elements in the environment. There was provided little or no purposing on the part of the learner. In procedures this movement continued the tendency toward atomism which was inherent in the idea of the earlier analytical psychology influenced by science.

Learning as conceived today by many of the frontier thinkers in education is a process affecting the organism as a whole. Of learning and its resulting changes Professor Kilpatrick writes:

When the organism faces a novel situation, old responses will not suffice. A new response is called for or failure confronts. If fortunate, the organism will contrive a response new to it and adequate to cope with the novel difficulty. Such a contriving we call learning. . . . The organism is different by the new response and all that it brings. Each act of learning adds a certain change and increment to the very structure of the organism itself. [39:5]

On the question of the way learning affects the organism as a whole, Woodworth states: "What happens at one point in the organism is never independent of, or without its influence upon, what is taking place at any other part of the organism." [77:110] Regarding the influence of the Gestalt movement upon the swing in point of view from the atomistic toward an organismic psychology, Woodworth says further:

As matters stand today, we certainly recognize in the Gestalt psychology a strong and valuable addition to the varieties of psychology [77:124] . . . ; it is a school of undeniable importance and may hold the key to the future. [77:15]

Position 3, learning as a process affecting the human organism in its total experience, has been set up under the guiding element, "The Curriculum Maker's Theory of the Way Learning Takes Place," to collect the findings for this point of view.

Position 4. A combination of positions was suggested where the examiner thought this would yield a fairer reaction to the materials being examined. Accompanying the suggestion, the request was made for an estimate of the per cent of the materials of each course which appeared under the various positions here set up.

DISCUSSION OF THE FINDINGS FOR "THE CURRICULUM MAKER'S THEORY OF THE WAY LEARNING TAKES PLACE"

Position 1

Learning as training . . . 4 per cent (approximately) of the 71 courses examined.

These conditions were found:

	Courses
Total number of courses under Position 1	3
Courses which made no mention of any point of view regarding the way learning takes place	3
Courses in which the curriculum materials showed much evidence of learning as training	3
Courses which used subject matter objectives as their professed philosophy	3
Courses which appeared under the two most formal positions set up for subject matter and showed no evidence of a guiding philosophy applied to the problem as a whole	3

Distribution by subjects of the courses of this group: All were in the field of arithmetic. There was evidence of a relationship between the subject matter objectives stated and the suggested experiences to carry out this point of view regarding the subject; but no guiding philosophy appeared for the total problem. Curriculum materials representing this point of view also appeared under the combination set for Position 4.

Position 2

Learning as the development of ideas through the assimilation of information . . . 11 per cent (approximately) of the 71 courses examined.

These conditions were found:

	Courses
Total number of courses under Position 2	8
Courses which placed the major emphasis upon information in their suggested educational experiences	8
Courses which showed subject matter objectives under the guiding element dealing with philosophy	5
Courses which stated some aspect of education as growth for their professed philosophy	3
Courses of this group of 3 which were consistent to some degree in applying their professed philosophy to the suggested experiences and appeared in the most informal position set up for subject matter	2
Courses which appeared in the position next to the most formal one set up for subject matter	6

Curriculum materials representing this point of view also appeared under the combination situation set up as Position 4. Distribution by subjects of the 8 courses in this group: general courses —2; social studies—3; art—3; arithmetic—0.

Position 3

Learning as a process affecting the human organism in its total experience . . . 49 per cent (approximately) of the 71 courses examined.

These conditions were found:

	Courses
Total number of courses under Position 3	35
Courses which used some aspect of the theory of education as growth for their professed philosophy and showed consistent effort to apply it to the suggested experiences	27
Courses which emphasized subject matter objectives as their guiding philosophy	8
Courses which appeared in the least formal positions set up for subject matter	28
Courses which appeared under the more formal positions set up for subject matter	7

Distribution by subjects of the courses in this group: general courses —8; social studies—18; art—7; arithmetic—2. The large number of social studies courses in this group adds further evidence that this field contributes in an outstanding degree to situations reflecting a range of worth-while experiences. The courses under this position showed the most consistent relationship between the professed philosophy and the suggested experience to carry out that philosophy. That 35 of the 71 courses examined appeared under this position is an item for curriculum workers to note with encouragement.

Position 4

A combination of any of the above positions . . . 35 per cent (approximately) of the 71 courses examined.

These conditions were found:

	Courses
Total number of courses under Position 4	25
Courses in which 70 to 75 per cent of the materials were estimated under Position 1 and 25 to 30 per cent under Position 2	3
Courses in which 60 to 75 per cent of the materials were estimated under Position 2 and 25 to 40 per cent under Position 3	6
Courses in which 70 to 90 per cent of the materials were estimated under Position 1 and 10 to 30 per cent under Position 3	16
Courses which showed subject matter objectives as their guiding point of view	11
Courses which appeared to some extent under the most formal position set up for subject matter	16
Courses which had a portion of their materials estimated as belonging under the least formal position set up for subject matter	18

Distribution by subjects of the courses of this group: general courses—6; social studies—7; art—4; arithmetic—8.

In the present state of change in the current curriculum thinking and the adjustment of the suggested educational experiences to meet this change, one may expect different aspects of the same course to appear in various positions on a scale from a formal to a well-balanced, progressive point of view. Learning as a process affecting the human organism in its total experience is one of the most promising elements in current educational thought. Its possibilities offer a challenge to all persons interested in the school's contribution to the educative process of the child. That this point of view confronts difficulties is evident. To square suggested curriculum experiences and procedures to carry the full import of this idea presents an interesting field for investigation and thought for several years to come.

SUMMARY

The findings for this guiding element show an interesting reflection of current curriculum thinking. Under Position 3 is found 49 per cent of the materials examined. In theory—if too infrequently carried out in practice—the curriculum maker declared his point of view on learning as the total experience. In some cases where the suggested experience was of the type to further this point of view, the opportunities for learning were limited by suggested procedures well freighted with the influence of the old faculty psychology. However, a declared position is a vantage point from which to make further progress of a more complete type.

The way learning takes place in the educative process is fundamental to the curriculum problem. Many influences concentrate at this point. Out of this welter of opinion and increasing investigation comes progress. Here is the arena where subject matter is defined. Here two concepts of learning stand out in sharp contrast to each other. They are embodied in the swing of the pendulum from a highly analytical concept to that of learning as a process affecting the human organism in its total experience. The courses which reflected the latter point of view were among those which showed the most consistent relationship between the professed philosophy and the suggested educational experiences to carry out that philosophy.

V. THE PLACE OF THE TEACHER

As Characterized in the "Guide for the Evaluation of Elementary Curricula" and Found through Its Use

How does this course provide for the use of the teacher?

A. *The teacher as a superimposed authoritarian.* In this position the teacher's task is to see that the curriculum—"subject-matter-set-out-to-be-learned"—is acquired by the learner. The teacher sets the assignment. The pupils learn, often by virtual memorization, to give back what is required. Almost all initiation and direction is in the hands of the teacher.

B. *The teacher as the most experienced member of the pupil-teacher group.* In this position the teacher functions in guiding the development of the child through a series of worth-while individual and group experiences embodying the opportunity for increasing self-direction. The initiation and direction of the various experiences are carried on through individual and group interests, through the teacher's awareness of lines along which progress seems desirable, and through pupil-teacher suggestions. Other elements contributing to this end are sharing, deliberate discussions—carrying provisions for many questions—and the opportunity for choice and decisions by the pupil-teacher group.

C. *The teacher as an adviser only in response to requests.* In this position the teacher serves wholly as an adviser in response to requests. These requests have arisen out of individual and group initiation and direction of activities. In this position there is the minimum guidance by the teacher, by the pupil-teacher group, or by the materials used.

Positions which this course may reflect on "The Place of the Teacher":

1. The teacher as a superimposed authoritarian.
2. The teacher as the most experienced member of the pupil-teacher group.
3. The teacher as an adviser only in response to request.
4. A combination of positions was suggested where the examiner thought this would yield a fairer reaction to the materials under consideration.

Positions, as defined above, found for "The Place of the Teacher" through the examination of 71 courses of study:

Position	Number of Courses
1	10
2	43
3	0
4 (A combination of 1 and 2)	18

Jury judgment agreement with the writer's evaluation of curriculum materials through the use of this guiding element . . . 92 per cent (approximately).

The steadily increasing influence of a biological philosophy and the numerous findings in the field of psychology have formed the background for and made possible the amazing growth reflected in the numerous phases of the child development movement. In response to these influences many aspects of the curriculum problem are centers of the controversy customary to most change in educational thought. No single aspect is being more conspicuously influenced than the one under discussion in this section. Out of the conflict of thought progress has been made. The role of the teacher is being gradually re-defined.

No single guiding element underlying the curriculum problem exists independently. This is especially true of one as important as "The Place of the Teacher." While the focus of attention emphasizes the main features of this element, the thorough interpreter is aware of the complexity of influences involved, the existence of some degree of overlapping with the other guiding elements used, and the many inter-relationships. Each of the various elements herein used, as a possible guide for curriculum experiences, exerts its influence upon the others and in turn is influenced by them. Among those which seem to be most sensitively interdependent are the two dealing with the role of the teacher and that of subject matter. Both in their relationship to the guiding philosophy used and to each other this interdependence is apparent. In setting up the guiding elements to collect these findings, in the results obtained, and in their interpretation these two aspects of the curriculum problem appear inextricably bound up. This relationship should be kept in mind as necessary to an understanding of the point of view used in the discussion of "The Place of the Teacher."

UNDERLYING ASPECTS ON WHICH THESE FINDINGS WERE COLLECTED

A briefly outlined background of the various positions used under this vital and changing guiding element should assist in understanding the findings obtained.

The traditional point of view regarding subject matter leaves no choice of the role the teacher must play. "Subject-matter-set-out-to-be-learned" implies some one to see that it is done. Memorization to give back what is required follows. The learner has little or no opportunity for initiation and direction. This concept of subject matter and this function of the teacher are well established in the curriculum thinking of many persons in education as well as in the minds of the majority of laymen. These concepts give way only to intelligent and co-operative consideration of the problem as a whole. In the extreme form this position assures the status quo and carries the possibility of minimum growth for all concerned. Position 1 has been set up to seek evidence on this point of view.

In the concept of education as growth the part that experience plays in the educative process creates a new role for the teacher. Here the learner reacting to his environment—the physical, the social, the esthetic—and carried on by the inward driving force of his own purpose needs a wise and understanding type of guidance. This is necessary to attain for the learner the richest possible meanings from his present experiences, to capitalize the best in his cultural inheritance, and to insure the extension of his horizon. Here, the teacher as the most experienced member of the pupil-teacher group may guide child growth through a series of individual and group experiences. Regarding this point of view Bonser says:

> This conception of education as personal-social growth through the interaction of personality and environment conditions the interpretation of "The teacher as a guide, not a task-master" . . . To guide their natural development requires that the teacher be trained to help the children to conduct efficiently all kinds of activities by which wholesome growth is promoted. [5:248]

Under this point of view evidence was sought that the teacher, as the most experienced member of the pupil-teacher group, guides child growth in the manner defined under position 2.

In making provision for evidence from the full range in points of view, position 3 was set up as the other end of the scale from position 1. Little or no guidance was emphasized under this position. This was done because the question of the kind and degree of guidance is one of the crucial elements in determining the role of the teacher. If position 3 is interpreted as intended, the child of elementary school age would be limited in the possible richness of his experiences and the extension of his interests. Initiation and direction are potent elements in the educative process. In the opinion of the writer much careful thought on wise ways of developing these elements needs to be centered here. Neither a superficial interpretation of the guiding philosophy used nor even the worthy attempt to get away from the teacher-dominated type of situation should be allowed to limit conditions tending toward well-balanced growth for the child. This point of view is taken to guard and capitalize initiation and direction through wise pupil-teacher guidance. No measure of these elements should be lost in their contribution to growth through lack of encouragement or the undernourishment of a promising interest. The guidance situation set up under this position might easily develop as one aspect in the well-rounded provision of position 2. This might occur while individual and group interests of a short-lived nature were being worked out, or as an exploratory means for the observation of child interests. However, when position 3, with little or no guidance, is considered as a *total* point of view it does not carry full provision for capitalizing all the elements which contribute to rich and ever-widening experiences with increasing self-direction for growing children.

This question of the type and degree of guidance, with its sensitivity to the point of view used regarding subject matter, is one around which the conflict between the progressive and the conservative elements in education largely centers. It is in the field of guidance—pupil-teacher, teacher, or materials—that some well-intentioned proponents of progressive education have frequently failed to capitalize for children all the values inherent in the experience-situation. Whether in private or public schools the commendable attempt to get away from the traditional teacher-dominated type of situation, with its subject-matter-set-out-to-be-learned, should receive full credit. However, the movement has not always reflected a vision of the problem as a whole nor the needed study of its various elements. Allowance for the necessary experimentation to translate an idea into procedure should be granted. Beyond this point there is reflected, too frequently, an inadequate acquaintance with the point of view on guidance which is presented in the professed philosophy and there is often evident a lack of attention to the fundamental laws of child development. These conditions have contributed to impractical and limiting procedures. Some of the procedures have frequently been defended by a pseudo-interpretation of the Dewey philosophy. Such an interpretation carries the possibility of preventing the well-balanced development of children. It has often failed to command the respect of the layman and has furnished fuel for the critics. All persons interested in the school's fullest contribution to the educative process of the child should concentrate on a wiser interpretation of the element of guidance at this weak point, so that the pendulum of opinion may not swing back toward the traditional teacher-dominated position.

Lack of guidance by the teacher is just as unfortunate at one end of the scale which measures teacher participation as is extreme adult domination and insistence on reproduction of models of perfection at the other end. The teacher must be able to see and develop educative possibilities in the child and in the environment. [59:iv]

With respect to this important question of guidance Dewey writes:

There is a present tendency in so-called advanced schools of educational thought . . . to say, in effect, let us surround pupils with certain materials, tools, appliances, etc., and then let pupils respond to these things according to their own desires. Above all let us not suggest any end or plan to the students; let us not suggest to them what they shall do, for that is an unwarranted trespass upon their sacred intellectual individuality. . . . Now such a method is really stupid. For it attempts the impossible, which is always stupid; and it misconceives the conditions of independent thinking. There are a multitude of ways of reacting to surrounding conditions, and without some guidance from experience these reactions are almost sure to be casual, sporadic and ultimately fatiguing, accompanied by nervous strain. . . . (The implication that the teacher is the one and only person who has no "individuality" or "freedom" to "express" would be funny if it were not often so sad in its outworkings.) [22:439]

These three positions, then, embody the underlying elements used in setting up guiding lines to collect the findings for "The Place of the Teacher." The role of the teacher becomes increasingly important.

DISCUSSION OF THE FINDINGS FOR "THE PLACE OF THE TEACHER"

Position 1

The teacher as a superimposed authoritarian . . . 14 per cent (approximately) of the 71 courses examined.

These conditions were found:

	Courses
Total number of courses under Position 1	10
Courses which showed the role of the teacher largely predetermined by subject matter selected in advance to be learned	10
Courses which showed little or no provision for choice on the part of the learner	9
Courses which showed provision for pupil-teaching planning	0
Courses which showed bare "subject matter" outlines	8

Courses which used subject matter objectives as their guiding philosophy	8
Courses which appeared in the most formal position set up under subject matter	8

Distribution by subjects of the 10 courses in this group: general courses—5; social studies—1; art—1; arithmetic—3.

On the whole the courses in this group under the position "the teacher as a superimposed authoritarian" showed formal subject-matter-set-out-to-be-learned. The curriculum content had been almost wholly determined in advance. It provided little or no initiation or direction on the part of the learner and carried no opportunity for pupil-teacher planning. The professed philosophy and the suggested educational experiences outlined were in terms of subject matter, in the limited sense. The role of the teacher was practically thrust upon her by the type of curriculum experiences suggested.

The following limitations to the teacher's fullest service appeared in a course in this group: "It is the duty of the teacher to test pupils' knowledge of work done in the preceding grades . . . to guide and direct with close attention home study and reading . . . The teacher's daily program should be posted in the classroom and rigidly followed." [2:1] This interesting bit of instruction to teachers appeared in an art course: "The teacher presents the subject but has it developed by the student." [57:5] If carried out, these instructions would prevent the learner from having several of the most important aspects of the educative experience, limit the services of the teacher to the child, and determine her role to a large degree. "The Place of the Teacher" and the concept used regarding subject matter are sensitively interdependent.

Position 2

The teacher as the most experienced member of the pupil-teacher group . . . 58 per cent (approximately) of the 71 courses examined.

These conditions were found:

	Courses
Total number of courses under Position 2	43
Courses which showed provision for varying estimated per cents of the elements ascribed to this position	43

Courses which showed definite provision for experiences in
pupil-teacher guidance   38
Courses which made provision for the type of experience in
which this element was implied   5
Courses which suggested discussion periods   28
Courses which emphasized the teacher's freedom of choice
in using suggested curriculum experiences   34
Courses which emphasized pupil participation in the choice
of curriculum experiences   23
Courses which used some aspect of the theory of education
as growth for their guiding philosophy   27
Courses which used this last mentioned philosophy and
showed the application of it in the suggested experiences   24
Courses which appeared in the least formal position under
subject matter   20

Distribution by subjects of the 43 courses in this group: general
courses—10; social studies—17; arithmetic—4; art—12.

It should be gratifying to all persons concerned with the element
of well-balanced guidance to note that the major portion of the
findings for this guiding element appeared under position 2 de-
fining "The Place of the Teacher" as the most experienced member of the pupil-teacher group. That the techniques for carrying
out this point of view need perfecting is admitted by most persons
in the field. The growth to this position, from a fairly widespread
teacher-dominated one at the beginning of the movement for less
formal schools, will be approved by many elementary workers. It
should be' guarded and extended by all.

The following points of view on guidance appear in the courses
of this group:

Guidance on the part of the teacher is essential. Skillful leadership will
permit the children much leeway for initiation and many opportunities
for choosing. It will also guide them out of desultory, shallow discussion
by timely suggestions for reading, experimentation, and investigation as a
means of solving their problems. [43:3]

This course suggested many possible experiences for carrying out
this point of view. Another course of this group shows, under "The
Teacher's Part," that "The teacher needs to be thoroughly conversant with all that is known about the development of habit, and
to use her knowledge with utmost intelligence and patience." [1:16]
The same course suggests to the teacher: "To learn how to be a
partner rather than a director." [1:20] A recent state course,

included as one of the special group in the plan of research for this study, makes the following statement: "The plan should be altered by teacher and children as the work progresses." [75:27] Another city course says: "The teacher becomes the guide." [70:7] Another course offers this guidance: "During the work period the teacher will study individual children and will guide the work to keep it on a high plane." [67:34]

Position 3
The teacher as an adviser only in response to request . . . o per cent of the 71 courses examined.

In setting up this position emphasizing little or no guidance only through response to request, it was expected that few courses of the elementary level for the public schools would appear in this group. The provision for a combination of positions under this guiding element apparently exerted an influence in the situation. A range of opinion was somewhat provided for outside the more extreme provision under position 3. Aspects of experiences listed under position 2 reflect position 3.

Position 4
A combination of positions 1 and 2 . . . 28 per cent (approximately) of the 71 courses examined.

These conditions were found:

	Courses
Total number of courses under Position 4	18
Courses which had 60 to 90 per cent of their materials estimated under Position 1	10
Courses in this group of 10 which appeared under the two most formal positions set up for subject matter	7
Courses which appeared in less formal position under subject matter	3
Courses in this group of 10 which expressed some aspect of the theory of education as growth for their guiding philosophy	6
Courses of the latter group which were consistent with their expressed philosophy in the role forced upon the teacher by their suggested experiences	2

Distribution by subjects of the 10 courses in this group: general courses—3; social studies—o; art—1; arithmetic—6.

	Courses
Courses which had the larger per cent of their materials estimated under Position 2	8
Courses of this group of 8 which expressed some aspect of education as growth as their guiding philosophy	5
Courses which appeared in the two least formal positions set up for subject matter	5

Distribution by subjects of the 8 courses in this group: general courses—2; social studies—4; arithmetic—1; art—1.

The same sensitivity of relationship between the role of the teacher and the concept used regarding subject matter seemed apparent throughout the various positions under this guiding element, "The Place of the Teacher." Further points of view on this important aspect of a current educational problem: "A teacher is the one vested by society with responsibility to guide the child's growth. . . . She must be one who is, herself, growing." [47:281] With respect to helping the child think for himself, one authority says:

One of the questions which takes on new importance is the place of the teacher. Her role is of very great significance. What is her part in providing situations and conditions which will stimulate the child to think for himself? How can she help him to see the facilities of the school, of his home and community, and to learn how to use them? [59:111]

Bonser's insight gives to the teacher a thrilling role:

Teachers are gradually learning how to evoke and direct the interests and capacities of children, to give freedom and expression to their creative ideas and feelings. . . . Children are responsive to the tactful guidance of teachers who themselves feel an impulse to see the minds of their pupils creatively express themselves. [5:242]

The teacher's part in making the curriculum experiences sufficiently challenging to command the respect of the learner is glimpsed by one whose opinion reflects first-hand contact with the eager spirit of the growing child. "The teacher is responsible for seeing that as far as possible the day is filled with delightful work, worthwhile work, hard work." [31:28]

SUMMARY

Investigation continues to reveal "The Place of the Teacher" as one of the pivotal elements in the curriculum problem. The concept of the teacher reflects a condition which needs further careful attention. It is evident that progress has been made when the findings show that 58 per cent of the materials considered the teacher as the most experienced member of the teacher-pupil group.

The inter-relationship of each guiding element to the total body of the guiding elements used has been mentioned elsewhere. Among those which seemed to be most sensitively interdependent were the two dealing with the role of the teacher and that of subject matter. The question of the kind and degree of guidance is a central problem under this guiding element and offers a rich field for critical thinking. The role of the teacher as the most experienced member of the pupil-teacher group appeared most consistently in the materials in which the relationship between the professed philosophy and the suggested educational experiences was most apparent.

VI. THE CHOICE OF THE CURRICULUM EXPERIENCES

As Characterized in the "Guide for the Evaluation of Elementary Curricula" and Found through Its Use

How were the curriculum experiences of this course chosen?

A. *Chosen in advance by adults.* In this type of course all experiences and materials have been outlined in advance by adults. There is little or no provision for choice on the part of the learner.

B. *Chosen by the teacher and pupils.* Guided by large objectives, the teacher and pupils choose the experience jointly.

C. *Chosen by the learner.* The learner, individually or as a member of the pupil group, may choose the experience independently unless the help of the teacher is requested.

Positions which this course may reflect on "The Choice of the Curriculum Experiences":

1. Chosen in advance by adults.
2. Chosen by the teacher and pupils.
3. Chosen by the learner.

Positions, as defined above, found for this much debated element in the curriculum problem, "The Choice of the Curriculum Experiences," through the examination of 71 courses of study:

Position	Number of Courses
1	7
1 and 2	33
2	25
2 and 3	6
3	0

Jury judgment agreement with the writer's evaluation of the choice of curriculum experiences . . . 92 per cent.

Who is to choose the curriculum experiences? This question is outstanding. A long and animated controversy has centered around this aspect of the curriculum problem. It has grown apace with the increasing recognition of the curriculum as a major educational responsibility. During the period of this recent growth in the curriculum-interest to the proportion of a nation-wide concern, three major influences, with their attendant contributions and limitations, have been reflected.

These major influences are frequently considered as the traditional, the scientific, and that resulting from the philosophy of dynamic growth. The traditional forces viewed the school from the starting point of fixed boundaries of subject matter. The source of this influence centered largely in the national committees. Their decrees regarding subject matter exerted a tremendous influence upon curriculum content, textbooks, and subsequent educational thought. This influence paralleled, as to time, the contribution of several of the advanced thinkers toward cutting across subject matter partitions and building the learning experience around interest centers. These two elements—subject matter of the fixed boundary type and experiences growing out of interests—appeared in opposition. Various phases of these two curriculum areas still furnish fuel for much of the current controversy in the field. The scientific approach to the curriculum problem was criticized for becoming immersed in its techniques, stressing the study of social needs, and giving little attention to child growth. The protagonists of the philosophy of dynamic growth are said to have centered their thought upon the child to such a degree that they ignored the complex social life surrounding it.

The limitations of these earlier tendencies are beginning to give way to a better relationship between the school curriculum and

American life. Current needs are being evaluated for possible directing elements. Problems of contemporary life appear more frequently in curriculum materials. The social values of suggested experiences are given increasing prominence. There is growing recognition in the current literature of the character of each stage of child development and the need to adjust the curriculum experiences so they will contribute to it. There is evidence of the beginning of a general movement from a formal position toward a less formal one in the current curriculum materials. Against this background the important question, "The Choice of the Curriculum Experiences," will be considered.

UNDERLYING ASPECTS ON WHICH THESE FINDINGS WERE COLLECTED

Under position 1, *Chosen in advance by adults*, all experiences and materials have been determined in advance. There is little or no opportunity for choice, decision, or consequent responsibility on the part of the learner. This is practically subject-matter-set-out-to-be-learned. Under this position the learner consumes, largely by memorization, what is set before him. The test of his success is as narrow as his task; he must give it back. There is little or no consideration of child development and the shaping of experiences to contribute to this end.

Position 2, *Chosen by the teacher and pupils*, has been set up under this guiding element to glean quite a different type of experience-situation from that provided under the foregoing position. Guided by large objectives, the teacher and pupils choose the curriculum experiences jointly. The degree of pupil participation implied is some indication of other important elements inherent in this type of experience.

Under this position, a combination of positions 2 and 3, and under position 3 as well, it is implied that provision will be made to have the various experience-situations of the curriculum grow out of the learner's interests and past experiences as frequently and as richly as possible. This is necessary in order to furnish connections of learning and provide better opportunities for the integrated growth of the learner both within himself and in relation to his environment.

Position 3, *Chosen by the learner*. This position is set up so that the learner, individually or as a member of the pupil group, may choose the experience independently unless help is requested from the teacher or pupil-teacher group. This is intended to portray phases of any functioning program of experience-situations rather than a total program with no provision for any pupil-teacher or teacher guidance throughout.

DISCUSSION OF THE FINDINGS FOR "THE CHOICE OF THE CURRICULUM EXPERIENCES"

Position 1

Chosen in advance by adults . . . 10 per cent (approximately) of the 71 courses examined.

These conditions were found:

	Courses
Total number of courses under Position 1	7
Courses which showed the curriculum experiences chosen wholly in advance and of the subject-matter-set-out-to-be-learned type	7
Courses which stated a guiding point of view for the curriculum as a whole	0
Courses which stated subject matter objectives for their guiding point of view	5
Courses which appeared under the most formal position set up for subject matter	7
Courses which showed practically no opportunity for choice on the part of the learner	7

Distribution by subjects of the 7 courses in which the choice of the curriculum experiences were chosen in advance by adults: general courses—1; social studies—1; art—1; arithmetic—4.

In curriculum materials of this type there is no recognition of the vital need for the various learning activities to grow out of the learner's interests and past experiences, so that rich connections may be built up. This point of view in the choice of the curriculum experiences also fails to capitalize the possible contribution that meeting many experience-situations, vital to the child, make to the total educative process.

A combination of positions 1 and 2

This position combines position 1, *chosen in advance by adults,* and position 2, *chosen by the teacher and pupils . . .* 46 per cent (approximately) of the 71 courses examined.

These conditions were found:

	Courses
Total number of courses under a combination of Positions 1 and 2	33
Courses which showed 60 to 90 per cent of their materials estimated as coming under Position 1, and 10 to 40 per cent under Position 2	28
Courses which showed 75 to 90 per cent of their materials estimated under Position 2, and 10 to 25 per cent under Position 1	5
Courses which showed varying estimated amounts of provision for choice of the curriculum experiences on the part of the learner	33
Courses which used subject matter objectives as their guiding point of view	10
Courses which stated both a guiding philosophy for the curriculum as a whole as well as specific aims	23
Courses which stated a professed philosophy for the curriculum as a whole and showed consistent effort to apply it to the suggested experiences	16
Courses which used some aspect of education as growth as their professed philosophy	14
Courses which appeared largely in the most formal position set up for subject matter	7
Courses which appeared in the most informal position set up for subject matter	8
Courses in which a portion of their materials were estimated in the most informal position set up for subject matter	14

Distribution by subjects of the 33 courses under the combination of Positions 1 and 2: general courses—9; social studies—11; art—2; arithmetic—11.

The courses of this group offered more opportunity for choice of the curriculum experiences on the part of the learner than those under Position 1.

As the courses in this group showed a higher per cent of their materials estimated as making provision for the choice of the curriculum experiences on the part of the learner, the evaluation given to the suggested experiences under the guiding element dealing with subject matter moved from the most formal toward the most informal position. The courses which stated their professed philosophy as some aspect of educational growth and applied it to their suggested experiences showed more provision for the choice of the curriculum experiences on the part of the learner. These courses showed more provision for experience-situations.

Position 2

Chosen by the teacher and pupils . . . 35 per cent (approximately) of the 71 courses examined.

These conditions were found:

	Courses
Total number of courses under Position 2	25
Courses which made provision to some degree for teacher-pupil participation in the choice of the curriculum experiences	25
Courses which stated subject matter objectives as their only guiding point of view	5
Courses which stated a guiding point of view for the curriculum as a whole and subject matter objective as well	20
Courses, of the latter group, which showed a consistent effort to apply their professed philosophy to the suggested experiences	14
Courses which appeared in the least formal position set up for subject matter	17
Courses which appeared to some extent in the position next to the most formal one under subject matter	8

The distribution by subjects of the courses under Position 2 of this guiding element: general courses—4; social studies—10; art—10; arithmetic—1. As provision for teacher and pupil participation in the choice of the curriculum experiences increased, the type of suggested experiences moved toward the least formal position estimated under subject matter.

A combination of positions 2 and 3

This position combines position 2, *chosen by the teacher and pupils* and position 3, *chosen by the learner.* Under it were found 8 per cent (approximately) of the 71 courses examined.

These conditions were found:

	Courses
Total number of courses under the combination of Positions 2 and 3	6
Courses which showed statements of a guiding philosophy as well as subject matter objectives	6
Courses which showed consistency between their professed philosophy and the suggested experience-situations to carry it out	6

Courses which showed the most provision for teacher-pupil
   choice of the curriculum experiences   6
Courses in which the materials were estimated under the
   most informal position set up for subject matter   6

The distribution by subjects of this group of courses under the
combination Position 2 and 3: general courses—1; social studies—
4; art—1; arithmetic—0. The distribution of courses by subjects
has, so far, reflected that where a predominance of social studies
courses, art courses, and a certain type of general course based
upon a program of experience-situations have occurred in a group,
their materials have been consistently estimated as coming under
the most informal position dealing with subject matter. An element
in these courses was the provision—to varying degrees—for the
choice of the curriculum experiences by the teacher and pupils.

Position 3

Chosen by the learner. No courses appeared, wholly, under this
position. This was no doubt due to the fact that position 3 was
available under a combination of positions 2 and 3. This position,
as set up under the guiding element dealing with the choice of the
curriculum experiences, was interpreted as meaning that the learner
received no guidance—unless requested—from the pupil-teacher
group, the teacher, or from the guiding objectives set up for the
curriculum.

The findings under this guiding element showed that the courses
which stated their professed philosophy for the curriculum as a
whole and showed specific objectives made the most consistent
provision for choice on the part of the learner. These same courses
had their materials estimated as coming under the two most informal
positions set up for subject matter. The majority of these courses
showed the most application of their professed philosophy to the
suggested experience-situations.

Provision for "The Choice of the Curriculum Experiences" appeared in various ways in a number of the courses examined. One
course, which showed many opportunities for participation on the
part of the learner in this important function of choosing the experiences, stated the following:

These unifying projects offer every opportunity for individual choice
of activity and hence have the advantage of placing the child in situa-

tions where he voluntarily undertakes a share in group work. . . . Within certain limits teachers and pupils should be given a large degree of freedom in choosing and organizing the particular unit experiences which they will enter into in any grade. [1:iv]

From another course:

We have tried to make it flexible enough that each teacher may recognize and adapt the learning situations which will best promote the continuous growth of her own pupils. [13:7]

From a state course included in the special group, as previously listed in the plan of research:

Freedom should be allowed for the teacher to organize instruction around the purposeful experiences of children. [75:15]

From the same course:

The plan should be altered by the teacher and children as the work progresses. [75:27]

Advanced thinkers advise that it is well to have the experience-situations of the curriculum grow out of the child's interests and background of constructive experiences, to the greatest extent possible, so that rich learning connections may be formed. It seems reasonable, then, to urge that this promising area for making these connections, "The Choice of the Curriculum Experience," be fully capitalized in the interest of the learner and enriched through wise guidance.

SUMMARY

How the curriculum experiences are to be chosen is one of the crucial points of the total curriculum problem. Here is centered much discussion and varying opinion. This element, together with the role of the teacher, the curriculum maker's theory of the way learning takes place, and the nature of subject matter are all inextricably bound together and exert a vital influence upon the type of curriculum experience which the school is making available to the child. Among a number of influences centering in the choice of the curriculum experiences are the traditional, the scientific, and that resulting from the philosophy of dynamic growth. All are involved in the beginning of a general movement from a formal position toward a less formal one.

The findings under this guiding element show an interesting movement from the position in which the curriculum experiences are wholly chosen in advance by adults toward the position in which they are selected by the teacher-pupil group with respect to tentative guiding lines.

As the courses examined made provision for choice of the curriculum experiences by the teacher and pupils, the estimated position of the materials under the guiding element dealing with subject matter moved over from the most formal toward the most informal position. The courses which made the most provision for teacher-pupil choice showed the greatest inter-relationship between their professed philosophy and the suggested educational experiences.

VII. THE RELATIVE IMMEDIACY OF THE EXPERIENCE TO THE CHILD

As Characterized in the "Guide for the Evaluation of Elementary Curricula" and Found through Its Use

What position does this course show regarding the relative immediacy of the experience to the child?

A. *The experience very remote.* This position uses situations well outside the child's range of interests. The subject matter is usually of the "set-out-to-be-learned" type, superimposed, largely the memorization of facts and with little or no effort at building interests.

B. *The experience within the child's mental, imaginative environment, through his range of interests and appreciation, but outside his immediate physical environment.* This type of experience capitalizes the child's imagination, utilizes meanings derived from past first-hand experiences, and usually results in enriching and extending his interests.

C. *The experience, immediate and first-hand, drawn from the child's proximate environment and having much social significance for him.* This type of experience-situation is very rich in possibilities for growth in behavior. It affords opportunity for choice and decision on the part of the learner, with its end usually vitalized by a life situation. Through its possibility for enriching meanings, this type of experience affords the best if not the sole means for practice in critical thinking.

Positions which this course may show on "The Relative Immediacy of the Experience to the Child":

1. The experience very remote.
2. The experience within the child's mental, imaginative environment, but outside his immediate physical environment.
3. The experience drawn from the child's immediate environment. A combination of positions was suggested under this guiding element.

Positions, as defined above, found for this highly important element, "The Relative Immediacy of the Experience to the Child," through the examination of 71 courses of study:

Position	Number of Courses
1	13
2	8
3	30
4 (A combination of positions 2 and 3)	20

Jury judgment agreement with the writer's evaluation of the immediacy of the experiences to the child . . . 89 per cent.

Most persons conversant with the records of the elementary school during the past twenty-five to thirty years will admit that for the country as a whole the emphasis has been upon the traditional point of view regarding the curriculum experiences. Passing on to the children of the period a body of accepted subject matter, frequently defended as the accumulated inheritance of the race, has been the dominant note. So far as the school's contribution to the child's total educative process was concerned, learning has been throughout the major portion of the new century the acquisition of isolated facts. A generation of exposure to a philosophy that has consistently stressed child development is having a marked effect upon this deeply intrenched traditional point of view. This has been especially evident during the last decade. The emphasis of this philosophy of experimentalism upon the all-round growth of the child is creeping into the suggested curriculum experiences. The phenomenal advance of a number of aspects of the early child study movement, with the recent outstanding contributions in the field of mental hygiene, join their influence to that of the philosophical thought, and these forces are helping to place the child, rather than subject matter, at the focus of interest. As these influences gain in area and as better techniques for their application are worked out by good teachers in the laboratory of the classroom, the nature of the curriculum experiences may be expected to move from that of the traditional subject matter type over toward a predominance of those experiences which are so connected with the child's interests and background that they are vital to him. Meanwhile the present status of this element should be interesting to note.

UNDERLYING ASPECTS ON WHICH THESE FINDINGS WERE COLLECTED

Under position 1, *The experience very remote,* an extreme traditional point of view is set up. Situations well outside the child's range of interests are largely used. The "set-out-to-be-learned" type of subject matter predominates. Learning, under this position, is largely the memorization of facts. The experiences of the child are rarely capitalized and there is little or no effort to build up possible connections of learning.

Position 2, *The experience within the child's mental, imaginative environment, through his range of interests and appreciation, but outside his immediate physical environment.* Too frequently the child's rich imaginative ability finds little opportunity for its rightful play. This rich field should receive more careful study and provision in the curriculum experiences than has hitherto been made. This type of experience carries possibilities of capitalizing and further developing the child's imagination. It utilizes meanings derived from past first-hand experiences. It is reasonable to assume that it carries possibilities of enriching and extending interests.

A combination of positions composed of 2 and 3 was set up for the purpose previously mentioned.

Position 3, *The experiences, immediate and first-hand, drawn from the child's direct environment and having much social significance for him,* has been set up under this guiding element to provide experience-situations rich in possibilities for growth in behavior. Curriculum experiences of this type afford opportunity for choice and decision on the part of the learner. Since they are usually vitalized by being drawn from life situations, they enrich meanings and offer excellent opportunities for practice in critical thinking.

This latter type of experience has always been fundamental to the educative process of the child. It is increasingly important that the school should make provision for this direct type of experience for the learner since the complexity of our modern industrial life has isolated the child in the home from so many of the experiences of vital social significance to him. According to Riley:

> The usual school has been so set apart . . . so isolated from the ordinary conditions and motives of life, that the place where children are sent for discipline is the one place in the world where it is most difficult to get such experience. Contrast with this the old days when the household was practically the center in which were carried on all the typical forms of individual occupation. The clothing worn was not only made in the house, but the members of the household were generally familiar with the shearing of the sheep, the carding and spinning of the wool, and the plying of the loom. In short, the entire industrial process stood revealed, from the production on the farm of the raw materials, till the finished article was actually put into use. Not only this but practically every member of the household had his own share in the work. . . . It was a matter of immediate and personal concern even to the point of actual participation. [62:291]

DISCUSSION OF THE FINDINGS FOR "THE RELATIVE
IMMEDIACY OF THE EXPERIENCE TO THE CHILD"

Position 1

The experience very remote . . . 18 per cent (approximately) of the 71 courses examined.

These conditions were found:

	Courses
Total number of courses under Position 1	13
Courses which showed 90 per cent of their materials estimated in this position	11
Courses which had their materials estimated wholly under this position	2
Courses in which the curriculum experiences were chiefly of the subject-matter-set-out-to-be-learned type	13
Courses having 5 to 10 per cent of their material in the position next to the most formal one under subject matter	5
Courses which showed subject matter objectives for their guiding point of view	13
Courses which stated a point of view for the curriculum as a whole as well as subject matter objectives	1
Courses which showed a consistent relationship between their professed philosophy and the suggested experiences	2

The distribution by subjects of the 13 courses under the position in which the experience was very remote to the child: general courses —2; social studies—o; art—o; arithmetic—11. In the courses of this group there was little or no evidence of the curriculum experiences being within the child's range of interests. The major portion of the stated, or implied, experiences was distinctly of the superimposed type.

Position 2

The experience within the child's mental, imaginative environment, through his range of interests and appreciation, but outside his immediate physical environment . . . 11 per cent (approximately) of the 71 courses examined.

These conditions were found:

	Courses
Total number of courses under Position 2	8
Courses which had 75 to 90 per cent of their materials estimated under this position	8
Courses which showed both a statement of a guiding point of view and subject matter objectives	5
Courses which showed only subject matter objectives	3
Courses which showed the full range from the formal to the most informal position set up for subject matter	8

Many of the curriculum experience-situations listed under this position dealt with child-life in other lands, pioneer life in this country, aspects of creative experience especially in the field of the arts, and experiences in the field of literature. This position provided for the type of experiences which are drawn largely from an imaginative environment. Although the group was small some provision for this element appeared under the combination of positions 2 and 3.

Distribution by subjects of the 8 courses which provided experiences within the child's mental imaginative environment but outside his immediate physical environment: general courses—o; social studies—8; art—o; arithmetic—o. The findings under this position reflect the need of more provision for the type of experience which gives fuller play to the learner's imagination. This valuable element should be utilized for its further development as fundamental to creative experience and as a means for extending and enriching experiences.

A combination of positions 2 and 3

This position combines position 2, *The experience within the child's mental, imaginative environment, through his range of interests and appreciation, but outside his immediate physical environment,* and position 3, *The experience, immediate and first-hand, drawn from the child's proximate environment and having much social significance for him.* Under this combination position were found . . . 28 per cent (approximately) of the 71 courses examined.

These conditions were found:

	Courses
Total number of courses under a combination of Positions 2 and 3	20
Courses which had from 20 to 40 per cent of their materials estimated under Position 2, and from 60 to 80 per cent under Position 3	12
Courses which had portions of their materials estimated under all three positions	8
Courses which showed statements of a professed guiding philosophy for the problem as a whole and subject matter objectives	16
Courses which stated subject matter objectives only	4
Courses which showed a consistent effort to apply their professed philosophy to the suggested experiences	11
Courses which stated a guiding point of view for the curriculum as a whole but showed little or no application of it to the suggested experiences	5
Courses which had their materials estimated in the most informal position under subject matter	10
Courses in which the materials were estimated in the position next to the most informal one	5

Distribution by subjects of the 20 courses in the combination position 2 and 3 under the guiding element, "The Relative Immediacy of the Experience to the Child": general courses—5; social studies—2; art—10; arithmetic—3. As the estimated amount of the materials increased under position 3, the subject matter evaluation moved toward the most informal position set up for that guiding element.

Position 3

The experience, immediate and first-hand, drawn from the child's proximate environment and having much social significance for him . . . 42 per cent (approximately) of the 71 courses examined.

These conditions were found:

	Courses
Total number of courses under Position 3	30
Courses which showed statements of a guiding point of view for the curriculum as a whole and specific objectives for the subject under consideration	25
Courses which stated subject matter objectives only	5
Courses which stated a guiding philosophy, specific objectives, and showed consistent application of their professed philosophy to their suggested experiences	16
Courses which had all or a portion of their materials estimated in the most informal position set up for subject matter	23
Courses which had their materials estimated under the position next to the most informal one set up for subject matter	7

Distribution by subjects of the 30 courses under position 3 of "The Relative Immediacy of the Experience to the Child": general courses —8; social studies—15; art—5; arithmetic—2.

The largest per cent of the courses in this group appeared under position 3. These courses showed more of their materials under the most informal position dealing with subject matter. More courses in this group showed a statement of a guiding philosophy as well as specific objectives relative to the subject in question. More evidence was found of a consistent relationship between the various elements of the professed philosophy used and the suggested experiences to carry out that philosophy.

Upon the vital significance in the immediacy of the experience to the child one course of this group says:

> The child's home life, his play and games, his hobbies and projects, his studies of nature and his activities in the community are the things in which he is most interested because he is a part of them, and our art problems will be very real ones if we manage to have them arise from these sources. They must be child problems and we must plan and judge the result of these problems from the standpoint of the child instead of the adult. [41:5]

This important aspect of the school's possible contribution to the total educative process through rich and immediate experience-situations of vital significance to the child is summed up by Bonser:

> All about are the raw materials for making the school work educative. The children are all alive with the capacities, the impulses, the activities,

the interests, and the urges with which to start. The community life with its homes, its occupational activities, its applied science, its geographical and historical connections with the world, present and past, its amusements, its music, its libraries, its churches, its local government—everything is at hand to bring the school and the activities and problems of life together in vital relationship for the education of the children. Education means increasingly participating in the activities of life. It never ends. [5:7]

SUMMARY

The difference between the findings of 18 per cent under position 1 and 42 per cent under position 3 of this guiding element shows a trend toward a type of curriculum experience that is vital to the child. As provision for the immediacy of the experience to the child increased, statements of a point of view to guide the curriculum as.a whole appeared more frequently. The courses which made provision for this type of experience showed more frequent inter-relationship between the professed philosophy and the suggested educational experiences. The imaginative environment of the child should receive its merited attention. Also, too frequently, rich imaginative ability finds little opportunity for its rightful play.

The type of curriculum experiences offered is at the focus of attention largely through the influence of a philosophy which emphasizes the all-round growth of the child and recent contributions to the field of mental hygiene. The need is increasingly apparent for the experiences to emerge from the learner's interests, to build further interests to extend his horizon, and to enrich meanings by drawing upon life situations which are vital to the child. This type of experience represents the other extreme from subject-matter-set-out-to-be-learned. It also affords the best if not the sole means for testing practical thinking.

VIII. PROVISION FOR LEARNING THROUGH FIRST-HAND EXPERIENCES

As Characterized in the "Guide for the Evaluation of Elementary Curricula" and Found through Its Use

Does this course emphasize learning through first-hand experiences by:

A. The use of a rich and varied program which embodies many challenging individual and group experience-situations providing opportunities for emphasizing learning through first-hand rather than vicarious experiences? This aim is realized through the continuous utilization of vital social situations in the immediate environment.

B. Provision for opportunities to respond to a wide range of challenging materials?

C. Provision for freedom, with respect to the immediate group and other groups, to explore, manipulate, and experiment?

D. Provision for much "doing" through the expression of ideas in concrete form in response to individual interests and group enterprises in which there is embodied continuous opportunity to practice self-direction and group participation?

E. Provision for sharing the responsibility of decisions?

Positions which this course may show on "Provision for Learning Through First-Hand Experiences":

1. Little or no provision for first-hand experiences.

2. Some provision for first-hand experiences inherent in the suggested outline, but little emphasis given to their use.

3. Definite provision made for many first-hand experiences in the suggested program.

Positions, as defined in the foregoing passage, found for this fundamental element of the curriculum problem, learning through first-hand experiences, by the evaluation of 71 courses of study:

Position	Number of Courses
1	15
2	14
3	42

Jury judgment agreement with the writer's evaluation of "Provision for Learning Through First-hand Experiences" . . . 98 per cent.

The reader is asked to keep in mind, as necessary to the discussion of the findings for this guiding element, the vital inter-dependence between the nature of the curriculum experience and the method involved. In case there is a tendency to consider learning through first-hand experiences as method only, and hence not wisely included in these guiding elements, it is here stated that while the aspect of method implied is fully recognized it is the nature of the curriculum experience—its possible first-handedness—that is to receive the major emphasis in this discussion.

It is quite apparent that the nature of the experience—the subject matter so-called—largely determines the method involved. Curriculum content of a static nature has built up its type of method. Each, content and method, contributes to the other. A curriculum program planned for inherent dynamic values must of necessity have the element of experiencing as its central tenet. This fact forces content and method to be unusually inter-dependent in the case of learning through first-hand experiences. Most educators will admit that the problem of developing wise guiding lines for the choice of dynamic curriculum experiences and better techniques to carry out the basic element of experiencing offers a challenging field for much thought and experimentation. Of the relationship between the type of subject matter and the method involved Taba says:

. . .; there is an intimate connection between subject matter and an adequate method of its study. A certain type of subject matter demands a certain approach and certain tools of study. The static outlook developed a method that was suitable for the subject matter as defined by this outlook. It is time for the dynamic outlook to formulate its own tools of research. [72:42]

UNDERLYING ASPECTS ON WHICH THESE FINDINGS
WERE COLLECTED

A brief discussion of the underlying principles on which this guiding element was set up should assist in a fairer interpretation of the findings on this vital aspect of the curriculum problem, "Provision for Learning Through First-Hand Experiences."

The fundamental aspect of this guiding element is experiencing. There is no assumption that vicarious experiences are not present to some degree in many phases of a dynamic program. However, the type of curriculum content under consideration in this section emphasizes learning through first-hand experiences.

That learning through the inherent activities in many first-hand experiences is in keeping with child nature is assured by an authority recognized for his provision of a wide variety of rich, first-hand, learning situations. Bonser says:

If you would know whether the school work is in harmony with the nature of the child, contrast the free, restless, untiring activity of the child of this age when left to himself with the artificial regime of the school with its blocking of all activity, with the damming up of the impulsive sense currents which must now be controlled by the utilization of inhibitive centers yet undeveloped, with the suppression of tendencies whose expression in free, unhampered activity is nature's only means of developing that strength and breadth of foundation necessary to the development of the more refined movements and activities of later life. [5:190]

. . .

In nature study and science, the planning and development of school or home gardens, studies of the habits of birds finding out the values and uses of various kinds of trees in the school community, . . . making a study of . . . ways of supplying water to homes, . . . a study of heating and fuel . . ., weather records, prevailing winds, and kinds and amounts of precipitation are all enterprises which require investigation and some measure of invention. No one knows the answers to the questions raised in advance. They cannot be gotten in books, although books will be helpful in answering them. They all require first-hand original inquiry. . . . In the pursuit of these activities, imagination, discrimination, accuracy of observation, and judgment are all stimulated and developed. Surely one can see how such studies differ from assigning materials in books to be memorized and recited—how they stimulate enthusiasm and effort, and how they evoke the inventive and creative abilities of children. . . . Books will be read with definite purpose and interest to help carry on the inquiries. More will be truly learned than if all study had been from books alone. We learn best only that which we really experience. Books are a help in all learning through experience, but they cannot be a substitute for first-hand experience. [5:245]

Three positions have been used to assist in the evaluation of current curricula through the application of this vital guiding element, "Provision for Learning Through First-hand Experiences." Position 1 gleaned information on the type of curriculum material which made little or no provision for this important element. Position 2 sought information regarding the type of materials which had first-hand experiences inherent in their suggestions but gave little emphasis to their use. Position 3 is provided to collect the findings from curriculum materials which have made definite provision for this valuable factor in the curriculum problem. The underlying aspects discussed and the three positions defined were the chief guides used for the collection of these findings. The reader is requested, however, to keep in mind that content and method are sensitively inter-dependent. The first-handedness of the experience is here stressed. The method is inherent.

DISCUSSION OF THE FINDINGS FOR "PROVISION FOR
LEARNING THROUGH FIRST-HAND EXPERIENCES"

Position 1

Little or no provision for first-hand experiences . . . 21 per cent
(approximately) of the 71 courses examined.

These conditions were found:

	Courses
Total number of courses under Position 1	15
Courses which showed little or no provision for learning through first-hand experiences	15
Courses which stated a point of view to guide the curriculum as a whole, listed specific objectives, and showed little evidence of applying their professed philosophy to the suggested experiences	4
Courses which used subject matter objectives as their guiding point of view	11
Courses in which the major portion of the material was estimated under the most formal position set up for subject matter	15
Courses in which the element of first-handedness was not evident in practically any of the materials listed	15

The distribution of subjects of the 15 courses which made little or
no provision for learning through first-hand experiences: general
courses—3; social studies—2; art—2; arithmetic—8. These courses
as a group offered little or no opportunity for the type of first-hand
experiencing which is set up under this guiding element. There was
little apparent relationship between their stated point of view to
guide the work as a whole and the suggested experiences.

Position 2

*Some provision for first-hand experiences inherent in the suggested
outline but little emphasis given to their use* . . . 20 per cent (approximately) of the 71 courses examined.

These conditions were found:

	Courses
Total number of courses under Position 2	14
Courses which stated a guiding point of view, used specific objectives also, and reflected a consistent effort to apply their professed philosophy to the suggested experiences	6
Courses which stressed subject matter objectives	8
Courses in which the materials appeared in the two most formal positions set up for subject matter	8

Courses in which some of the materials showed elements of first-hand experiences but did not record their use for this approach to learning	8
Courses which had their materials estimated in the position next to the most informal one set up for subject matter	6

The distribution by subjects of the 14 courses in this group: general courses—3; social studies—4; art—2; arithmetic—5. Most of the possible first-hand experiences appeared in the field of the social studies, general courses of the less formal type, and art courses.

The situation revealed in this group of courses is another of the kind which should receive careful consideration from all educators. When the first-hand type of experience is considered most effective for learning by the best current opinion, it should be a challenge to all concerned with the enrichment of the curriculum content to capitalize to the fullest all possibilities of this type.

Position 3

Definite provision made for many first-hand experiences in the suggested program . . . 59 per cent (approximately) of the 71 courses examined.

These conditions were found:

	Courses
Total number of courses under Position 3	42
Courses which showed a statement of a guiding point of view for the total curriculum, as well as specific objectives	36
Courses, of this latter group, which used some aspect of the theory of education as growth for their professed philosophy	28
Courses which showed only subject matter objectives	6
Courses which showed consistent effort to apply their professed philosophy to the suggested experiences	22
Courses which had all or a portion of their suggested experiences estimated as coming within the most informal position set up under subject matter	32
Courses which had their materials estimated in the two positions midway between the most formal and the most informal setup for subject matter	10

The distribution by subjects of the 42 courses which made definite provision for many first-hand experiences: general courses—9; social studies—18; art—13; arithmetic—2.

It should be encouraging to persons advocating this type of curriculum experience to note that by far the larger per cent of the materials of the 71 courses examined were estimated as belonging to the position which made definite provision for many first-hand experiences. As the estimated amount of provision for first-handedness in the learning experience increased, the location of the curriculum materials under the criterion for subject matter moved over from the most formal toward the most informal position. As the provision for first-hand experiences increased, the relationship between the professed philosophy and the suggested experiences became more apparent.

The fact that 59 per cent of the courses in this group had their materials estimated as making provision—in varying degrees—for learning through first-hand experiences carries interesting implications. It seems reasonable to conclude that growth in a philosophy of education which emphasizes experiencing as fundamental to learning is exerting its influence upon this phase of the curriculum experiences. Stress upon the first-hand type of experience rather than a predominance of vicarious experiences appears in much of the literature in the field. The activity movement, to which learning through first-hand experiences is fundamental, shows a steady gain in favor as reflected by the number and type of the suggested experience-situations recorded to serve some form of that growing demand. This growth is due to the fact that a program of experiencing serves a biological need of the growing child. At present this movement is hampered by the need for developing more adequate techniques and it is frequently limited by the type of organization which fails to recognize its central tenets. In the opinion of the writer its provision for learning through first-hand experiences, together with its opportunities for practice in social living, makes it a vitalizing force awaiting further and more skillful application to the enrichment of the school's contribution to the child's total educative experience.

On the importance of first-hand experiences in learning, one course in this group comments:

Psychologists agree that the basis for all learning is in the concrete experience. The question of the amount of such experience needed in the classroom is an unsettled one. [18:35]

This point of view is an interesting reflection of sensitivity on the part of the curriculum maker to current opinion in the field of psychology accompanied by the traditional influence regarding the place of first-hand experiences in the classroom. An arithmetic course says:

> The work at all times is connected with the personal interest of the children. This is so important that a teacher is justified in omitting drill and other formal work while she takes her class to a cafeteria, to a store, to a station, to a bank in order to build up experience. [55:11]

A course which showed much provision for many rich, first-hand experiences prefaced its suggestions with the following statement as a portion of the guiding philosophy, which was consistently applied throughout its materials:

> We believe that the method of education is experiencing. That through these intrinsically worthwhile experiences the child should grow in his power to interpret the physical world and the society in which he lives. [1:iii]

In some of the courses of this group, which made definite provision for many first-hand experiences, there appeared many possibilities and suggestions for experience-situations. Lists of "Possible Activities" appeared. Much attention was given to capitalizing and enriching the environment. Suggestions were made for "Things the Children Might Like to Do." Well-utilized excursions were given their rightful educational emphasis. Provisions for creative experience were evident. Opportunities for choice of the curriculum experiences by the teacher and pupils were common. A list of "Suggested Activities" or of "Possible Experiences" was frequently followed by the advice to "Use only if they were vital to the immediate situation." In a number of instances the teachers and children were advised to choose, substitute, and enlarge upon all suggested experience-situations.

Of first-hand experiences in the curriculum Taba comments:

> The curriculum cannot be regarded as a dead and summative body of all the materials, experience and activities contained in the educational process. It is a living whole, comprised of experience actually going on in school. As such it is what it becomes in practice. Its content is identical to the content of the actual experience of the learner. [72:243]

SUMMARY

The findings for this guiding element reflect the early stages of a trend which carries possibilities of more dynamic learning situations. In 41 per cent of the materials examined, under positions 1 and 2, either little or no provision was made for first-hand experiences or they failed to emphasize the use of any opportunities which were inherent in their suggested experiences. Such a condition should receive further investigation and careful study. That 59 per cent of the materials examined show definite provision for learning through first-hand experiences should be noted as progress made.

In the discussion of this guiding element, "Learning Through First-Hand Experiences," the question of the method implied is fully recognized. However, it is the nature of the curriculum experience—its possible first-handedness—that is the major concern. It is easily apparent that the nature of the experience—the subject matter so called—largely determines the method involved. Each, content and method, contributes one to the other. Curriculum content of a static nature has built up its type of method. A program planned for its inherent dynamic values must of necessity have the element of experiencing as its central tenet. Content and method are sensitively inter-dependent in the case of learning through first-hand experiences. As provision for this element appeared in the materials examined for this study, statements of a guiding philosophy for the problem as a whole increased, and the courses of this group showed more consistent effort to apply their professed philosophy to the suggested experiences.

IX. ·PROVISION FOR CREATIVE EXPERIENCE

As Characterized in the "Guide for the Evaluation of Elementary Curricula" and Found through Its Use

Does this course show provision for creative experience through:

A. The use of a rich, well-balanced variety of stimuli provided for meeting a wide range of individual interests, with resulting promise of releasing creative impulses? Such stimuli are inherent in interesting materials and challenging experience-situations of all types, calling forth responses in other fields as well as expression in the arts.

B. Provision for an atmosphere which encourages creativity? Such a condition is promoted by a wholesome, sympathetic environment which stimulates and encourages creative experiences for the individual and the group, with frequent opportunities for sharing and enjoying results both with the school and with the home.

Positions which this course may reflect on creative experience:

1. No recognition of or provision for creative experience, as such.
2. Some provision inherent in the suggested experiences, but little emphasis given to the utilization of these opportunities.
3. Definite provision for a rich program of creative experiences.

Positions, as defined above, found for this important guiding element, "Creative Experience," through the examination of 71 courses of study:

Position	Number of Courses
1	20
2	21
3	30

Jury judgment agreement with the writer's evaluation of "Provision for Creative Experience" . . . 89 per cent.

At the outset of this discussion attention is called to the terminology herein used for this newly recognized but important element in the educative process. It is intended that the term "creative experience" shall convey a more inclusive concept than that usually conveyed by the term "creative expression." The two terms are frequently used for much the same type of experience, while the latter may well be applied to one phase of the former. This more limited concept arose largely from the fact that in the early period of the recognition of this element much of the so-called "creative expression" fell in the field of the arts. Creative music, creative art, creative verse, creative rhythm appear most frequently in the early literature on this subject. It is natural that the aspect most commonly emphasized at the time should color the terminology used until the more inclusive concept—creative experience—could be built up. It is here intended that creative experience shall include thought itself, any instance of significant thinking, that is, any experience in which the individual is faced with a new situation, or problem, for which old responses are inadequate and for which he must work out a new solution. Whatever the form which the expression may take—that of human behavior, of physical construction, of music, of rhythm, or of art—it is in the meeting and solving of the new situation with its appropriate expression that the creative act has resulting growth to the individual. "Using the experience one has, in new ways, to gain more experience is creative." [5:242]

UNDERLYING ASPECTS ON WHICH THESE FINDINGS WERE COLLECTED

It will perhaps contribute to a clearer interpretation of the findings on this important aspect of the curriculum experiences to clarify briefly this guiding element as set up for collecting evidence from printed curricula on the "Provision for Creative Experience."

The importance of a rich, well-balanced environment with a wide range of stimuli stands out. The human organism is constantly reacting to its surroundings. Whether it be the physical, the social, or the esthetic aspect which is immediately uppermost, this reaction is going on continuously. In working out ways to meet the new situations that arise learning takes place. In order to provide for learning through creative experience a well-balanced environment, rich in stimuli and many challenging experience-situations to meet a wide range of interests, becomes a crucial need. In such an environment there is a vast storehouse of possible learning situations. With the broader concept of creative experience and with the growing acceptance of the fact that all individuals create, to some degree, a rich environment furnishes both the stimulation trigger to set off the creative impulse and at the same time the medium in and through which the creative act goes on. Thus, while the impulse lies available within the individual, the other pole of the creative experience lies in the environment. Individuals, of course, differ. The stimulus which may serve to set off the creative impulse in one individual may not affect another. For this reason the school— and the home to an increasing degree—should surround the child with an environment of rich, well-balanced stimuli of all types which will set off and draw out his creative ability.

As an element of equal importance with rich stimuli, or as another phase of the same conducive environment for creative experience, is an educational climate in the school that encourages creativity. Rich stimuli would be largely lost to their fullest contribution, or at least greatly limited, if they were not enveloped in an atmosphere which encouraged their best utilization. These two elements then—a stimulating environment and an atmosphere of encouragement—were the basic elements used in setting up guiding lines for the collection of these findings.

DISCUSSION OF THE FINDINGS FOR "PROVISION FOR CREATIVE EXPERIENCE"

Position 1

No recognition of or provision for creative experience, as such . . . 28 per cent (approximately) of the 71 courses examined.
These conditions were found:

	Courses
Total number of courses under Position 1	20
Courses which recognized creative experience in their introductions or suggested experiences	0
Courses which stated subject matter objectives under the guiding element dealing with the philosophy	12
Courses which made no statement of a guiding philosophy	2
Courses which showed "Statements of a Point of View" to guide the curriculum as a whole and some slight application of them to the suggested experiences	6
Courses which appeared in the most formal position set up under the guiding element dealing with subject matter	14
Courses which appeared in a less formal position under subject matter and were the same courses which showed "Statements of a Point of View" to guide the curriculum as a whole	6

In general there was little provision for creative experience in this group of 20 courses. There was little evidence shown of a relationship between a guiding point of view and the suggested experiences.

The distribution by subjects of the 20 courses of this group which made "No Provision for Creative Experience": general courses—4; social studies—2; art—1; arithmetic—13. It seemed unusual that an art course should appear in this group. This was due to the fact that it was distinctly formal, was to be followed rigidly, and showed no provision for creative experience as here defined. It is interesting to note that social studies courses appeared less frequently, while arithmetic courses appeared in the largest number under this position.

The inclusion of arithmetic courses among the materials investigated for creative experience implies the broader concept of this element. In meeting and solving new situations the factor of number frequently enters. To the extent to which arithmetic is drawn from life situations and the relationship of a number fact, not merely the fact itself, is emphasized, will number function increasingly in creative experience. There is no assumption here that arithmetic will contribute, at the present, to this type of experience to the extent to which such fields as the social studies and the arts are now doing. Nor is the question of adequate skills here involved. It is, however, the conviction of the writer that as the number experiences of the curriculum are made increasingly dynamic, it is reasonable to expect the contribution from the field of arithmetic to creative experience to increase, with the number skills themselves becoming more effective through deepened meanings. According to the *Tenth Yearbook* of the National Council of Mathematics, creative experiences may call for many opportunities for number:

In the full development of most activities . . . arithmetic will be necessary many times. Here arithmetic serves as a tool or as a means to the solution of the larger purpose, rather than an end in itself. Arithmetic is a part of the process by which the child refines—resolves his problem. There is no forcing of artificial experiences in order to make opportunities for arithmetic, but whenever the situation functionally calls for arithmetic solution, it naturally comes into the activity. [48:88]

As the value of creative experience to the educative process continues to permeate curriculum material, a decrease in the per cent of courses showing no provision for this element may be expected to occur.

Position 2
Some provision inherent in the suggested experiences, but little emphasis given to the utilization of these opportunities . . . 30 per cent (approximately) of the 71 courses examined.
These conditions were found:

	Courses
Total number of courses under Position 2	21
Courses which showed some possibilities for creative experiences but gave little emphasis to their utilization for this purpose	21
Courses which made no mention of creative experience and	

showed few activities in which this important element was.
inherent 10
Courses which showed a fair range of activities in which
creative experience was inherent but gave little emphasis
to their use 11
Courses which showed no "Statement of a Point of View"
to guide the curriculum as a whole 10
Courses which showed some type of a guiding statement
for the total problem 11
Courses which appeared in the most formal position set up
under subject matter 5
Courses which appeared in the position next to the most
formal one set up under subject matter 16

It is interesting to note that courses showing no provision for creative experience appeared in the most formal position under subject matter.

Distribution by subjects of the 21 courses in this group: general courses—4; social studies—8; art—6; arithmetic—3.

The findings under this position of the guiding element, "Provision for Creative Experience," stand out as particularly challenging. That this element, so vital to the full development of the individual, was plainly inherent in the curriculum experiences and not fully capitalized by its recognition and use, should carry valuable implications to guide future curriculum efforts.

Position 3

Definite provision for a rich program of creative experiences . . . 42 per cent (approximately) of the 71 courses examined.

These conditions were found:

Courses

Total number of courses under Position 3 30
Courses which recognized the value of creative experience
and made provision for this important element 30
Courses which recognized creative experience in their "Statements of a Point of View" and showed provision for it
in the suggested experiences 24
Courses which stated their points of view on creative experience, made definite provision for it, and emphasized
the utilization of the opportunities to this end 21
Courses of the last-mentioned group which appeared under
the least formal position as set up for the guiding element
"Subject matter: How Thought of and How Accordingly
Used" 21
Courses which expressed some form of the theory of education as growth to guide the curriculum problem as a
whole 24

The concept of "creative expression" rather than "creative experience," as previously defined, showed in the major portion of the suggested experiences under this position. There was evidence of more relationship between the professed point of view and the suggested experiences in the courses which appeared in this position than in any other group under this guiding element.

Distribution by subjects of the 30 courses in this group: general courses—9; social studies—13; art—8; arithmetic—1. As the provision for creative experience became more apparent in the material examined, the number of social studies and art courses showed an increase in the group.

The following excerpts show examples of frequent inter-relationship between the professed philosophy and the suggested experiences to put this philosophy into practice:

We place eagerness to carry out creative ideas as more suitable for emphasis in the lower grades than skills. [1:18]

From the same course:

It is almost impossible for a young child to form a purpose in the absence of material things; for things stimulate the purpose. [1:8]

These statements were followed by the suggestion that the materials be

. . . bright and attractive to them, which means color and variety and things that offer opportunity . . . materials, tools, and books . . . easily accessible. [1:18]

Furthermore, the course revealed a clear relationship between the philosophy and the suggested experiences:

. . . Remember that the test for growth is not how well the idea has been expressed, but how many ideas the child has had and how readily he has expressed them. [35:41]

The above excerpts appeared in a course which was rich in suggested materials and experience-situations for creative learning.

The philosophy expressed in the following excerpts from another course was carried out by many suggested experiences:

Induce creative thinking by providing worth-while experiences. [74:4]

And from the same course:

[Make possible] growth in ability to do creative work. [74:21]

The two basic elements—a stimulating environment and an atmosphere of encouragement—underlie this criterion and have shaped its findings. Their importance is emphasized further in the following:

In so far as the environment is rich in experimental materials and in ideas the play of children progresses and takes on rich meanings. [7:210]

No matter how poor the early product the child must be encouraged to do more. [30:274]

Appreciate the child's "first effort." [35:41]

Provide much practice in dramatization because of the stimulation it affords to the creative impulse in language and to choice imagery. [13:39]

. . . ; there is no form of play that is as permanently and highly satisfying as is creative work. [1:13]

The more inclusive concept of creative experience as defined at the outset of this discussion is finding its way into frontier curriculum material. A Denver course included in this study carries this statement:

As the child reconstructs his experiences in the light of a new situation, creative learning is taking place. It is highly desirable that all learning partake of this characteristic since it is the natural expression of the individual in adjusting to his environment. [16:21]

A little child's work is creative if his contribution to a discussion, his portrayal of a character in dramatization, or his illustration of a story reflects something of his individual reaction to an experience or situation. [16:4]

One element has tended to confuse and to limit somewhat the early service of this newly recognized and promising aspect of the educative process, namely, the frequent over-emphasis on the product of the creative experience rather than on the opportunity for possible growth through the experience as a whole. While the product is not to be ignored and becomes important as the culmination of the experience, its chief value lies in its relation to the total experience and to the stimulation of further creative effort.

The recognition of the importance of creative experience in education is relatively new. The work and writings of Mearns, Coleman, Cizek, Rugg, and others have helped to build a wider interest. The proponents of a philosophy stressing the biological psychology have continuously advanced its possibilities as vital to growth. Of this important element in education Professor Kilpatrick says:

. . . All in some manner create, the few in high degree. Creation is peculiarly the work of the self and person as such. There can be no truer respect for personality than to expect and encourage creation. And creation enriches life. Nor is creation confined to "art." All life demands it and illustrates it. To join things in a new way so as to meet adequately a sensed situation of any nature whatever is among the most enjoyable of experiences, and the more meaningful the surer the joy. Every person's life abounds in such opportunities. To help find the promising places for creation, to help build the wish to create, and to help find the means of better creation—than these the educator has no higher duty. In creative work life has infinite possibilities. [39:16]

SUMMARY

The findings under positions 1 and 2 show that 58 per cent of the materials examined made no provision for creative experience or failed to emphasize the utilization of inherent possibilities. This fact may well challenge the attention of all persons interested in the fullest development of the growing child. The findings under position 3 show that 42 per cent of the materials made definite provision for creative experience. There should be a note of encouragement in this progress made.

The concept of "creative expression" rather than "creative experience," as defined elsewhere in this section, was used in the major portion of the curriculum materials examined by means of this guiding element. As the provision for creative experience increased, statements of a point of view to guide the curriculum as a whole appeared more frequently and the type of subject matter became more informal. In the courses which made definite provision for creative experience, as under position 3, there appeared more frequent inter-relationship between the professed philosophy and the suggested educational experiences to carry out this philosophy.

X. GROWTH IN INTELLECTUAL CURIOSITY

As Characterized in the "Guide for the Evaluation of Elementary Curricula" and Found through Its Use

Does this course encourage intellectual curiosity, through:

A. Wholesome provision for frequent group opportunities to present questions, share experiences, and discuss individual interests?

B. Provision in the suggested program for many challenging individual and group experience-situations which open new areas of information, enrich meanings, and extend interests?

C. Utilization of opportunities for stimulating further individual or group inquiry regarding possible leads growing out of the core experience?

D. Recognition and encouragement given to further inquiry by providing opportunities for sharing, evaluating, and enjoying results with both the school and the home groups?

Positions which this course may reflect on "Growth in Intellectual Curiosity."

1. No provision made, as such.
2. Some experiences provided for encouraging intellectual curiosity, but their use not emphasized.
3. Many experiences provided for encouraging intellectual curiosity, and emphasis given to their use.

Positions, as defined above, found for this vitalizing guiding element, "Growth in Intellectual Curiosity," through the examination of 71 courses of study:

Position	Number of Courses
1	12
2	41
3	18

Jury judgment agreement with the writer's evaluation of "Growth in Intellectual Curiosity" . . . 96 per cent. This agreement was obtained through jury judgment by having experienced persons in the field evaluate the same course of study.

As a background for the discussion of the findings for this guiding element, the reader is asked to give curiosity its rightful place of importance. It is a source of driving forces which exert a powerful influence upon the development of the individual and his possible contribution to society. Curiosity manifests itself early and if wisely directed by the parents through the early years it may become one of the most constructive and determining elements. It challenges the school and the home with the responsibility of its wise guidance.

. . . our task as physicians, educators, and parents is similar to that of the engineer. We must aid in the conversion and transformation of this energy so that the individual and mankind may benefit by it. Civilization owes its advance to the drive of curiosity. Wherever progress has been made, this trait has played an important role. Learning, knowledge, realization of the complex world we live in are all dependent upon its continuation. [68:73]

The elementary school stands with the home in a strategic position of opportunity for the constructive direction of this vital influence. Reflected largely as ceaseless investigation, curiosity is predominantly present in the growing child. Sad, indeed, for the learner is the type of school experience which sends him forth with a few mastered facts but with less of eager curiosity for new experiences than when he came. The responsibility of all persons interested in the full development of the child's potentialities—through the home, the school, and other agencies—may well be to make possible the type of experience-situations which capitalize and direct curiosity toward deepening and enriching present meanings and the building of ever wider and richer interests.

UNDERLYING ASPECTS ON WHICH THESE FINDINGS
WERE COLLECTED

Some clarification should be made of the various aspects on which this guiding element, "Growth in Intellectual Curiosity," was set up to collect evidence from printed curricula. This seems pertinent to assist in a fairer interpretation of the findings on this vital element.

The provision of opportunities to present questions stands out. First-hand acquaintance with children of elementary school age shows a marked tendency for eager, persistent questioning, investigation, and experimentation with the materials of their environment. This period ranks high in importance. The drive of eager curiosity has set the child a fundamental task. He must extend his investigation of the environment, orient himself in his social setting, and discover numerous generalizations for his use. It should be a matter of much concern to educators that too frequently the child's early eagerness diminishes and there is little evidence that his priceless native curiosity has been wisely recognized, encouraged, and guided toward broader interests. Much provision for questions must be made. The sharing of experiences is not only fundamental to social growth but a rich breeding ground for further worth-while questions. Here, in a social setting—vital to the child—he may gain the information important to him, grow in his ability to present worth-while questions, develop skill in participation, and have his horizon steadily extended.

This guiding element is set up with the assumption that the experience-situation type of curriculum content carries greater opportunities for capitalizing and directing the curiosity of the growing child than the traditional subject-matter-set-out-to-be-learned. In the experience-situation, both the individual and the group have the stimulating challenge of seeking the solution of a problem which is vital to them. Since the child must do his own growing, it is maintained that out of much experiencing in such a program there is possibility for growth. Experiences arise through which meanings are enriched, new areas of information are opened up, and interests are extended. Some practice is provided in the acquaintance with sources of information. The skills necessary to serve a growing intellectual curiosity are further developed. The wide variety of individual interests may be challenged by the various leads growing out of the core experience of the group or by worth-while individual interests from any source. Finally, intellectual curiosity thrives in an educational climate that recognizes its value by making continuous provision for worth-while experiences and emphasizing their further possibilities.

Many opportunities for sharing the various individual and group interests provide wholesome situations for evaluating and enjoying them. The utilization of the child's social group is an element of such influence that it should be considered basic to rich curriculum experiences. Both the school and the home should participate in sharing and enjoying the results which accrue from encouraging intellectual curiosity.

The foregoing underlying elements and the three positions here set up were the guiding lines used in collecting these findings on intellectual curiosity.

DISCUSSION OF THE FINDINGS FOR "GROWTH IN
INTELLECTUAL CURIOSITY"

Position 1

No provision made, as such . . . 17 per cent (approximately) of the 71 courses examined.

These conditions were found

	Courses
Total number of courses under Position 1	12
Courses which showed no recognition of intellectual curiosity either in statements of their guiding point of view or the suggested experiences	12
Courses which used subject matter objectives to express their guiding philosophy	7
Courses which stated a guiding point of view for the total curriculum and specific subject matter objectives	5
Courses, in the latter group, which showed evidence of applying their professed philosophy to their suggested experiences	4
Courses which appeared in the most formal position set up for subject matter	7
Courses which appeared in a less formal position set up for subject matter	5

Distribution by subjects of the 12 courses which showed no provision made, as such, for "Growth in Intellectual Curiosity": general courses—3; social studies—1; art—5; arithmetic—3. The materials in the courses of this group were largely of the traditional type of subject matter and, according to the content set up for this guiding element, failed to recognize the importance of intellectual curiosity.

Position 2

Some experiences provided for encouraging intellectual curiosity, but their use not emphasized . . . 57 per cent (approximately) of the 71 courses examined.

These conditions were found:

	Courses
Total number of courses under Position 2	41
Courses in which the materials showed inherent opportunities for encouraging intellectual curiosity but their use to this end was not emphasized	41
Courses which stated a guiding philosophy for the total problem as well as specific objectives	28
Courses, in the latter group, which showed a consistent effort to apply their professed philosophy to their suggested experiences	20
Courses which stated subject matter objectives	13
Courses which showed a portion of their materials estimated in the most formal position set up for subject matter	8
Courses which had their materials estimated as being wholly,	

or in part, in the most informal position set up under
subject matter 26
Courses which had their materials estimated between the
most informal and the most formal positions set up for
subject matter 7

Distribution by subjects of the 41 courses which showed some experiences provided for encouraging intellectual curiosity, but their use not emphasized: general courses—5; social studies—16; art—9; arithmetic—11. Social studies and arithmetic contributed the largest groups under this position. The estimated wide range of the materials of this group from the very formal to the most informal position, under subject matter, may be explained by this situation. A predominance of social studies courses in a group has usually moved the estimated position under subject matter over toward the most informal type. A predominance of arithmetic courses usually moved the estimated position over toward the most formal type.

Since the largest portion of the materials examined under this guiding element came within this position, there is need for the concerted attention of educators at this point in the curriculum problem. Advanced thinkers emphasize the vital influence of well-guided intellectual curiosity upon the development of the individual and his possible contribution to society. It is indeed unfortunate that opportunities to further conserve and direct the dynamic forces generated through curiosity should not be fully capitalized.

Position 3

Many experiences provided for and emphasis given to their use in developing intellectual curiosity . . . 25 per cent (approximately) of the 71 courses examined.

These conditions were found:

Courses
Total number of courses under Position 3 18
Courses which provided experiences planned to develop intel-
lectual curiosity and emphasized their use 18
Courses which stated both a guiding philosophy for the cur-
riculum as a whole and specific objectives 17
Courses which used subject matter objectives 1
Courses which stated some aspect of education as growth and
showed consistent effort to apply it to the suggested ex-
periences 16
Courses which had their materials estimated in the most in-
formal position under subject matter 17

Distribution by subjects of the 18 courses in this group: general courses—8; social studies—8; art—2; arithmetic—o. The social studies courses were among the majority. The general courses were of the type that provided many experience-situations. They stimulated curiosity through provision for individual and group investigation, deliberate questions, and experimentation.

As provision for encouraging intellectual curiosity increased, the type of subject matter moved from the most formal position toward the most informal one and the application of the professed philosophy to the suggested experiences became more apparent.

It seems evident that these findings on the vital element of intellectual curiosity add a further note of needed emphasis for the curriculum maker to that of the best current opinion. This aspect of the experiences which the school is offering to the child challenges attention. The importance of encouraging intellectual curiosity is advanced by leaders in educational thought. The findings under this guiding element show that the major portion of the curriculum materials, for the period of this study, did not emphasize the utilization of opportunities to encourage intellectual curiosity. This appeared to be the case even though the suggested experiences carried the possibilities—to some degree. This was the case even though the smaller portion of the curriculum materials, for the same. period, provided many experiences to further intellectual curiosity and emphasized their use to this end. These facts point to the need for further emphasis in the educational literature and increasing consideration, by curriculum makers, of the possibilities for individual development and social contributions which may result through encouraging intellectual curiosity.

One of the courses in this group reflected a point of view on guiding growth in intellectual curiosity. It asks: "Do they want to make return trips to find answers to their questions? Is there conversation and discussion resulting from genuine experience and thought provoking questions?" [1:23] This course showed many suggested experiences to carry out this point of view. Another course urges ". . . that the pupil have the opportunity to engage in many life-like activities which possess for him a maximum of meaning and purpose." [9:xiii] This course made provision for experiences, questions, discussions, and a climate of encouragement.

Another group of curriculum makers revealed their attitude on the importance of encouraging intellectual curiosity, as follows: "All activities should foster an inquiring, investigating attitude." [60:83] This point of view was consistently reflected in many suggested experience-situations found in their materials. The following statement appeared in another course: "We must assist our children to the point where they can and will think for themselves." [27:6] A course, among a special group included in this study, declares that "The teacher should encourage the pupils to search for materials in newspapers and magazines." [75:219] Another special course, under the heading "Observation and Discussion," points out that "This [the search for materials] is an effective way to create in children a keen active interest and stimulate their curiosity concerning the world about them." [52:23]

Martha Peck Porter, an outstanding contributor to the field of elementary education, writing for the teacher on this important aspect of learning, comments as follows:

. . . ; the children must not only be engaged in activities that are full of possibilities for learning; they must also be encouraged to constant curiosity. They will not know what interesting facts lie close to the things they are doing; the teacher must point the way. But if she encourages them to form the habit of looking below the surface of things, if she early shows them that curiosity is rewarded by new and interesting experiences, if she constantly helps them to reference material of all sorts and makes its use habitual, they will soon become conscious that valuable facts may be related to their activities, and that their own questions will bring these facts to light. That is why it seems to me that my main purpose must be that of encouraging an eager curiosity. [59:58]

SUMMARY

The findings under this guiding element may well arrest and hold the attention of all persons seriously interested in developing children. Under positions 1 and 2 there is recorded 75 per cent, approximately, of all the materials examined. These courses showed little or no provision for the direction of this dynamic element or failed to emphasize the use of opportunities inherent in the materials for encouraging it. Such a condition needs much investigation and well-studied correction. Under position 3, the fact that 25 per cent of the materials examined made provision for growth in intellectual curiosity shows that a start has been made.

Curiosity is a source of driving forces which exert a powerful influence upon the development of the individual and his possible contribution to society. It manifests itself early and, if wisely directed, it may become one of the most constructive and determining elements. The home and the school are both challenged with the responsibility for its wise guidance. Curiosity is predominantly present in the growing child. The home, the school, and other agencies should make possible the type of experience-situations which capitalize and direct curiosity toward deepening and enriching present meanings and the building of ever wider and richer interests. The courses which made provision for growth in intellectual curiosity showed more frequent statements of a point of view to guide the curriculum problem as a whole, and their materials were estimated in the most informal positions under subject matter. The relationship between the professed philosophy and the suggested educational experiences was more apparent.

XI. PROVISION FOR THE ENRICHMENT OF LEISURE TIME

As Characterized in the "Guide for the Evaluation of Elementary Curricula" and Found through Its Use

Does this course show provision for the enrichment of leisure time, through:

A. Exposure to a wholesome, well-balanced program of experiences which seem to appeal to a wide variety of interests and stimulate further individual and small group interests?

B. The recognition and encouragement of individual and group interests, arising either in the school or out of school experiences, through provision for sharing them for group enjoyment or entertainment?

C. The continued approval of constructive new interests, with the frequent expression of the most dominant ones at that particular period of development?

D. Encouragement, through individual and group approval, of growth in the skills necessary to pursue an outstanding interest and enjoy it increasingly?

Positions which this course may reflect on "Provision for the Enrichment of Leisure Time."

1. No provision for the enrichment of leisure time.
2. Some provision inherent in the suggested experiences, but little emphasis given to the use of these opportunities for the enrichment of leisure time.
3. Definite provision for many experiences contributing to the enrichment of leisure time.

Positions, as defined in the foregoing passage, found for this recently emphasized element in the curriculum problem through the examination of 71 courses of study:

Position	Number of Courses
1	12
2	32
3	27

Jury judgment agreement with the writer's evaluation of the provision made for the enrichment of leisure time . . . 98 per cent.

What of leisure time and its enrichment? Does this recently recognized element create the need for a change in the attitude of the American people?

The element of leisure time, carrying the necessity of making provision for its enrichment, has emerged from the social and economic conditions of American life within comparatively recent years. As a defined need pressing for attention, leisure time has come upon us rapidly. That this newly recognized element has its roots in certain conditions is apparent. That its permeation—to any degree—into our national life will necessitate an about-face in an attitude of long standing, cannot be overlooked.

To the pioneer American with a vast continent to conquer, the question of leisure time practically did not exist. All members of the family were busy from daylight until dark wresting a living from their frontier environment. Amusements there were, to be sure, but these largely grew out of some co-operative effort of the far-flung pioneer neighborhood to raise a house or barn, or the individual and group efforts to secure necessary food through hunting and fishing. During the long period when the young nation was achieving for itself the governmental, agricultural, and industrial development necessary for national security, the persistent effort toward these ends helped to build up an attitude of approval of the energy and drive necessary to accomplish them. These qualities gradually became typical of the American. Being busy, accomplishing things, overcoming difficulties, seeking some new adventure, making money, and playing the game were all phases of the so-called American drive. The self-made man stood out as a type. The so-called rugged individualist was a recognized success in his world of business but was frequently lost in handling any leisure time when conditions presented it.

During this period of development certain fundamental forces were at work. The results of their steady reshaping and realignment of various elements in American life have produced new and challenging conditions. The frontier has disappeared. Gigantic industrial developments have largely urbanized a population which was distinctly agricultural. Undreamed of advance in the field of science and mechanical appliances have touched every strata of American life. Industry has been taken out of the homes. Apprenticeships have disappeared. Various groups have joined in seeking better working conditions. The number of hours of labor have decreased with indications for further change pointing in the same direction. Economic conditions have forced many mothers into the various fields of industry. Consequently, important elements of home life have been changed for large numbers of children. Cities face the problem of inadequate play space. Mounting traffic accidents take heavy toll in the congested areas. The barriers of distance are still being overcome by thrilling conquests in the fields of transportation and communication. Commercialized amusements have a grip upon American recreational life. Much of the advance made in adult play is confined to favored groups and too often highly competitive. All these conditions create many new problems. None is more challenging than that of "Provision for the Enrichment of Leisure Time."

The American people as a whole must face the full import of this problem. That we now have leisure time without the training to use it wisely must be admitted. Its underlying principle runs counter to the well-established point of view on being busy, achieving, and making money. As a nation we must build an attitude—through experiencing—toward the importance of enriching interests and recreational activities as necessary in the life of every well-balanced individual. Conditions to make this possible are a necessary premise.

The role of education in relation to this important need stands out. The elementary school, working with the home, occupies a strategic position during the years when the foundation of habits and attitudes is being gradually laid. This need for the enrichment of leisure time has received recognition as a curriculum objective during the present decade. A start has been made. How widely is this problem of such tremendous personal and social influence receiving attention in the current curriculum materials? Further investigation of its present status should be of interest to curriculum makers and of some value as a guide to subsequent curriculum experiences.

UNDERLYING ASPECTS ON WHICH THESE FINDINGS WERE COLLECTED

Fundamental to the enrichment of leisure time is the early opportunity to begin the building of varied interests. Exposure to a wide range of experience-situations and an educational climate which surrounds the child with the encouragement to pursue his constructive individual interests should contribute to present and future leisure-time activities. The home, the school, and the most interesting features of the environment should be drawn upon to serve this end. Sharing interests for information and enjoyment is usually conducive to their growth. The development of the skills necessary for further investigation and for the fullest enjoyment of the individual's or group's particular interest is an important feature.

It seems pertinent at this point to call attention to another aspect of this important subject. The writer has found that where the school's program was of the experience-situation type and sufficiently dynamic to truly challenge the child's past experiences and imagination, many awakened interests carried over as leisure-time activities. Under such conditions children of elementary school age pursued, as highly recreational, tasks which the casual observer termed work. It also frequently occurs that many adults, whose school experiences at the same age were largely, if not wholly, of the subject-matter-set-out-to-be-learned type, do not recognize the child's participation in the various activities of an experience-situation program as serious gripping work to the learner and necessary to the solution of some problem vital to him. This is the traditional point of view resulting from a program which largely emphasized the memorization of a body of facts. It gives way slowly, although much of the current frontier thought calls attention to the effects of the learning which takes place through experiencing as far more vital to individual growth than the mere memorization of facts.

In addition to extending individual and group interests toward the enrichment of leisure time, it is possible to begin the building of an attitude toward truly interesting work that frequently raises it, during the most challenging stages, to the level of being chosen above other interests. This point of view should contribute to the enrichment of the individual's work rather than narrow the scope of his interests.

These underlying elements, together with the positions previously defined, were used as guiding lines to collect information regarding the enrichment of leisure time.

DISCUSSION OF THE FINDINGS FOR "PROVISION FOR THE ENRICHMENT OF LEISURE TIME"

Position 1

No provision for the enrichment of leisure time . . . 17 per cent (approximately) of the 71 courses examined.

These conditions were found:

	Courses
Total number of courses under Position 1	12
Courses which made no mention of the enrichment of leisure time and suggested no activities for this purpose	12
Courses which used subject matter objectives to express their guiding philosophy	10
Courses which made a statement of a point of view for the total curriculum problem, as well as subject matter objective, but showed little application of their professed philosophy to the suggested experiences	2
Courses in which the experiences were largely of the subject-matter-set-out-to-be-learned type	12
Courses which had their materials estimated under the most formal position set up for subject matter	10
Courses in which the materials were estimated under the position next to the most formal one set up for subject matter	2

Distribution by subjects of the courses which made no provision for the enrichment of leisure time: general courses—4; social studies—o; art—o; arithmetic—8. Besides making no provision for the enrichment of leisure time, this group of courses showed practically no opportunity for such elements as teacher-pupil choice of the curriculum experiences, the utilization and enrichment of the environment, or growth in intellectual curiosity. This group of courses showed little relationship between their professed philosophies and their suggested experiences.

Position 2

Some provision inherent in the suggested experiences, but little emphasis given to the use of these opportunities for the enrichment of leisure time . . . 45 per cent (approximately) of the 71 courses examined.

These conditions were found:

	Courses
Total number of courses under Position 2	32
Courses which showed a statement of a point of view and specific objectives	20
Courses which used subject matter objectives under the guiding element dealing with philosophy	12
Courses which showed consistent efforts to apply their professed philosophy to the suggested experiences	14
Courses which used subject matter objectives and had their materials estimated under the two most formal positions set up under subject matter	12
Courses which stated a guiding point of view for the total problem, used subject matter objectives, and had their materials estimated in the two most informal positions under subject matter	20
Courses which showed a consistent effort to apply their professed philosophy to the suggested experiences and had the major portion of their materials estimated in the most informal position set up for subject matter	14

Distribution by subjects of the courses under this position: general courses—4; social studies—8; art—12; arithmetic—8. The 32 courses examined for this position composed the largest group under this criterion. That the materials of these courses reflected possibilities in their suggested experiences but had little emphasis given to the use of these opportunities for the enrichment of leisure time, should offer a challenge to further curriculum efforts.

Position 3

Definite provision for many experiences contributing to the enrichment of leisure time . . . 38 per cent (approximately) of the 71 courses examined.

These conditions were found:

	Courses
Total number of courses under Position 3	27
Courses which showed some provision for the enrichment of leisure time	27
Courses which showed a statement of a guiding philosophy as well as specific objectives	25
Courses which used some statement of education as growth in their guiding philosophy for the curriculum as a whole	20
Courses which showed consistent effort to apply their professed philosophy to the suggested experiences	18
Courses which had their materials estimated wholly, or in part, under the most informal position set up for subject matter	17
Courses which had their materials estimated next to the most informal one set up under subject matter	10

Distribution by subjects of the courses which made definite provision for many experiences contributing to the enrichment of lesiure time: general courses—9; social studies—14; art—4; arithmetic—0.

As the provision for the enrichment of leisure time became more apparent throughout the three positions of this guiding element, the position of the materials under subject matter moved from the most formal position toward the most informal one. This covered a range from the subject-matter-set-out-to-be-learned type through the dynamic experiences of participating in the solution of some problem vital to the learner. In the latter, subject matter is interpreted as the total experience.

The wide range of suggested experiences to enrich leisure time, together with their wider range of possibilities, is reflected in such suggestions as the following: "Activities and Interests Growing out of the Units of Work"; "Excursions to Interesting Places"; "Things Children Might Like to Do"; "Sharing Books We Have Enjoyed"; "Dramatic Play"; "Exhibiting Our Best Pictures"; "Listening to Stories and Music"; "Learning Games"; "Our Pet Show"; "Sharing Hobbies"; "Making Things"; "Nature Experiences—Field Trips, Ways of Attracting Birds, Listening to the Rain, The Sky at Night";

"Holiday· Activities—Singing Carols to Our Friends and Shut-In People"; "Other Lands"; "Making Our Own Movies."

One course suggests encouraging the wise use of leisure time—

By helping the child to gain enjoyment and knowledge from the beautiful and good in art, music, literature, and the great out-of-doors. By aiding him to enjoy wholesome and worthwhile pleasure and recreation. By helping him find and develop his impelling avocational interest in life which will provide opportunities for self-expression or for creative effort. [29:1]

This point of view was carried out in many suggested experiences recorded in that course.

On the challenge of this problem, "Provision for the Enrichment of Leisure Time," former Commissioner of Education Cooper declares that:

Leisure time has come upon us rapidly. We are forced to find something for children and young folks to do. . . . What are our adult schools doing about these matters? What changes are our schools for minors making to keep step with the rapidly changing times? [49:283]

This important new need, which exists so widely in American life, has been created by those forces and conditions centering in and around our industrial development and the too rapid urbanization of society during this period. Overstreet sums up this problem:

. . . whatever the program may be that we plan for the future, we shall have to consider the wholeness of life. [56:25]

He says further:

Leisure that is to be worth the living must issue out of a work-life that is equally worth the living. This is the first principle which a decent civilization must premise. [56:19]

The same author discusses the wide range of possible interests to enrich leisure time:

There are the organic things—sunlight and clean air, the warm soil, running water, waving wheat in the fields, the call of birds. They are good even to think about. In some curious way they are interwoven with our life. [56:110]

Of our relation to our environment he says:

To shrink within oneself and away from one's surroundings is a defeated form of life. Hence a good philosophy will pre-suppose on the part of the individual an effort to transform what seems to be an alien environment into something that becomes understood and appreciated. [56:134]

Education is challenged to make its contribution to the pressing need for a wiser use of leisure time. This challenge concerns the entire educational program from the years of earliest childhood through adult life. This responsibility is continuous as long as the need exists. Education cannot escape it. Professor Kilpatrick declares that:

Wherever people need to learn in order to meet life, there education has a positive obligation. [56:127]

In meeting this need, it seems to the writer that education has the opportunity to perform a dual role. It is in the position to help lay the foundation for richer and wider interests for children, and in meeting this challenging need the interests of educators should be renewed and extended.

On a problem of such far-reaching influence, it would seem wise to realize the need, take stock of what has been done, and do much careful, critical thinking regarding all future contributions. Overstreet stresses the importance of such a course:

So with more free hours ahead of us, the time would seem propitious to take stock of ourselves and ask what we would really like to do with them. Free time can be a chance for us to invite our souls, or it can be one more chance for us to invite outsiders in to take charge of our souls. [56:171]

SUMMARY

This guiding element represents an educational need which has appeared as a central objective in the curriculum field within the past decade. Under positions 1 and 2 there appeared 62 per cent of the materials examined. These courses made no provision for the enrichment of leisure time or failed to emphasize the utilization of inherent possibilities. This condition may well claim the attention of all persons interested in the development of children. Position 3 shows that 38 per cent of the materials made provision for the enrichment of leisure time. It is encouraging to note that a definite trend in this direction is under way.

This new need reflects in miniature a stage of growth in American life. The problem of leisure time was recognized by incorporating the need in a central objective which was widely discussed within the past decade. Although the enrichment of leisure time has had this recognition, it has not yet permeated the curriculum materials to the extent which might be expected. With conditions as they are, the problem of leisure time becomes a vital one both to the growing child and the growing adult. Here is a factor contributing to richer living. As provision for this element increased, statements of a point of view to guide the curriculum as a whole appeared more frequently. In the same courses which made definite provision for the enrichment of leisure time, there also appeared more frequent relationships between the professed philosophy and the suggested educational experiences.

XII. SOCIALLY USEFUL WORK

As Characterized in the "Guide for the Evaluation of Elementary Curricula" and Found through Its Use

"Socially useful" is defined as work important to the community group, both adults and children, of which the child is a member. This work is to be *appropriate for the child at that age level* and not a superimposed adult task savoring of exploitation.

Does this course show provision, in part, for "Socially Useful Work" through:

A. The utilization of experience-situations of the "socially useful" type in which the experiences are more' distinctly physical than social?

B. The utilization of experience-situations of the "socially useful" type which have an obvious social element?

Positions which this course may show on "Socially Useful Work."

1. No provision for "socially useful" work, as such.
2. Provision for "socially useful" work through the utilization of experiences which are more distinctly physical than social.
3. Provision for "socially useful" work through the utilization of experiences which have an obvious social element.

Positions, as defined, found for this much needed guiding element, "Socially Useful Work," through the examination of 71 courses:

Position	Number of Courses
1	36
2	9
2 and 3	20
3	6

Jury judgment agreement with the writer's evaluation of the choice of curriculum experiences . . . 86 per cent.

What is meant by "socially useful" work in the fullest concept of this guiding element? Of what conditions and needs is this recently coined term the expression? Let us use care to give practice in group participation its rightful value in this experience as well as the work accomplished. Each is a vital part of a dynamic social experience.

It is important that the reader review, and possibly enlarge, his own concept of the term as a background against which these findings may be discussed. "Socially Useful Work" as here defined carries the implication of adults and children working together on something that is important enough to need to be done.

A brief review of the experiences that were available to the present-day adult group when they were of elementary school age would show a startling contrast to the experiences now available to their children. The child of that period not only observed but participated in many activities vital to the home and the community group. His school life furnished another type of experience. Rapid advance in the scientific and mechanical phases of modern life have created another set of conditions. The child of the present period is forced to have many vital experiences outside the home, or miss them entirely. He must look largely to the school to lead in making this possible. This institution has too often remained apart from the more vital activities of life so that a gap between the in-school and the out-of-school experiences too frequently exists. Under the persistent influence of a philosophy of experimentalism, which has emphasized participation in activities of social value, this gap is being studied and somewhat decreased. Progress has been made.

The child study movement recognizes the value of "socially useful" work. Industrial arts, as interpreted by Professor Bonser, enriches it. Better conditions for building an integrated personality are inherent in this type of experience. The value of adults and children working together on something that needs to be done is emphasized by an outstanding leader in educational thought:

We wish ultimately that schooling shall reach into life itself. . . . In that life the young will have opportunity at close association with the old.

. . . Learning of all kinds will be inherent, intrinsic in life processes.
[37:57]

UNDERLYING ASPECTS ON WHICH THESE FINDINGS
WERE COLLECTED

At the outset, it is stated that in the two types of "socially useful" work used in setting up this guiding element there is no implication that any experience-situation could be void of some degree of the social element. This use of the two types does not imply that one is wholly physical with no element of the social, or that the other is wholly social with no element of the physical. It is frequently true, however, that an experience-situation of the type which provides "socially useful" work may carry a predominance of experiences of one or the other type. This guiding element has been set up to seek information regarding the provision for "socially useful" work. These elements together with the positions, as previously defined, have formed the guiding lines upon which these findings were collected.

Position 1
No provision for "socially useful" work, as such . . . 50 per cent (approximately) of the 71 courses examined.

These conditions were found:

	Courses
Total number of courses under Position 1	36
Courses which showed no provision for "socially useful" work	36
Courses which stated a guiding point of view and used specific objectives	13
Courses which used subject matter objectives to express their guiding philosophy	23
Courses in which the materials were estimated under the two most formal positions set up for subject matter	23
Courses which had their materials estimated in three positions ranging from the most formal toward the most informal one set up for subject matter	13
Courses which showed consistent effort to carry out their professed philosophy in their suggested experiences	5

Distribution by subjects of the 36 courses which made no provision for "socially useful" work, as such: general courses—8; social studies—6; art—10; arithmetic—12. There is no assumption that some unemphasized aspect of the suggested experiences, listed in the materials of this group of courses, did not carry "socially useful" work. However, as defined by this guiding element, these courses were estimated as making little or no provision for this element.

Position 2

Provision for "socially useful" work through the utilization of experiences more distinctly physical than social . . . 13 per cent (approximately) of the 71 courses examined.

These conditions were found:

	Courses
Total number of courses under Position 2	9
Courses which used a statement of a guiding point of view and specific objectives to express their professed philosophy	8
Courses which showed a consistent relationship between their guiding philosophy and their suggested experiences	7
Courses which had their materials estimated as ranging from the most formal to the most informal position set up under subject matter	9

Distribution by subjects of the courses in this group: general courses—o; social studies—1; art—4; arithmetic—4.

These brief résumés of "socially useful" work appeared in the courses of this group: One of the needs of a community was a better attitude toward safety regarding fire and the use of preventive measures. Adults and children participated in experiences to accomplish this end. The suggested activities were appropriate for the age level of the children. Many co-operative experiences involving both adults and children were provided. At the request of the adults in a large school a lower grade group assumed the responsibility of handling the building mail through their postoffice. A community planned and assembled food for "A Thanksgiving Dinner." The necessary activities were participated in by adults and children who worked together both outside and inside the school.

A combination of positions 2 and 3.

Position 2, *Provision for "socially useful" work through the utilization of experiences more distinctly physical than social* and 3, *Provision for "socially useful" work through the utilization of situations having an obvious social element* . . . 28 per cent (approximately) of the 71 courses examined.

These conditions were found:

	Courses
Total number of courses under a combination of Positions 2 and 3	20
Courses in which 60 to 75 per cent of their materials were estimated under Position 2 and 25 to 40 per cent under Position 3	8
Courses in which 20 to 50 per cent of their materials were estimated under Position 2 and 50 to 80 per cent under Position 3	12
Courses which stated a guiding philosophy and specific objectives	16
Courses which showed a consistent effort to apply their guiding philosophy to their suggested experiences	15
Courses which showed a range from an intermediate position through the most informal one set up for subject matter	20

Distribution by subjects of the courses in this combination of positions 2 and 3: general courses—5; social studies—11; art—4; arithmetic—0.

The following are typical of recorded experiences which appeared in the courses of this group: The adults and the older children of the community collected and tested the soils of that locality. A series of community meetings were held to discuss and demonstrate what to do in an emergency and to hear the chief of police or the local policeman explain police services and the need of co-operative activities for protection and traffic safety. Adults and children of the community discussed and planned how recreation could be had for all at a minimum cost.

Position 3

Provision for "socially useful" work through the utilization of situations having an obvious social element . . . 8 per cent (approximately) of the 71 courses examined.

These conditions were found:

	Courses
Total number of courses under Position 3	6
Courses which showed a guiding point of view and specific objectives under the guiding element dealing with the philosophy	6
Courses which showed a consistent effort to apply their stated philosophy to the suggested experiences	6
Courses in which the materials were estimated in the two most informal positions set up under subject matter	6

Distribution by subjects of the courses which made provision for "socially useful" work through the utilization of situations having an obvious social element: general courses—2; social studies—4; art—o; arithmetic—o. "Socially useful" work of the type defined under position 2 appeared most frequently in the curriculum materials of the lower grades. "Socially useful" work of the type defined under position 3 appeared most frequently in the curriculum materials of the upper grades.

The following are brief records of "socially useful" work which appeared in the materials of this group: A representative community group of adults and children prepared and sang Christmas carols for their locality. A pageant was given by adults and children portraying the history of their community. Songs and dances were presented by various racial groups and learned by the community group. This experience was an aid to building a better inter-racial attitude. As a phase of a problem vital to a Southern community, the extermination of the boll weevil was furthered by the children learning and protecting the birds that are friends to the cotton farmers.

On the whole this important element had too little provision made for it in the curriculum materials. This condition existed in the same courses which presented various "Curriculum Units" for the social value of their content. The advance that is reflected where curriculum materials are evaluated for their social aspects should be noted with encouragement. However, "socially useful" work carries such possibilities of bringing a dynamic quality into the curriculum experiences that it should command much careful thought and investigation on the part of all educators.

It seems pertinent at this point to emphasize two elements in the consideration of all "socially useful" work for children of elementary school age. First, any exploitation of children for work and responsibilities which rightfully belong to adults runs counter to every principle and value inherent in this type of experience. Any such grave misuse of this dynamic element may be prevented by having the proposed experience carefully evaluated to determine whether it is *appropriate for the child at that age level*. Second, all experiences which are considered as "socially useful" work should be native to that particular situation. The need must grow out of the situation and the work must answer that need. On this aspect a recent contribution by Hanna advises that: "The project must be indigenous to the community which sponsors it, or it will wither for lack of vitality." [33:viii] This is the only guarantee for capitalizing the full range of values inherent in "socially useful" work which awaits doing through participation of the whole group—adults and children—of which the child is a member. Here is a real situation for practicing democratic living. It is only through such experiences that the growing individual gradually becomes aware of his part in a community and gains the techniques, through practice, for intelligent participation. Writing of the 4 H Clubs, Robbins reports: "These young people learn by doing. They do socially useful things. Early in life they acquire a sense of the community and their part in it." [63:27]

SUMMARY

"Socially Useful Work" promises dynamic values in the curriculum experiences which have not always been present. The gap between life within the school and life outside the school is bridged by co-operative group experiences. Numerous situations in which the growing individual may have practice in democratic participation are provided as he works on a problem vital to the group— adults and children—of which he is a member. It is only through such experiences that the child may become aware of the community of which he is a part and of his place in the life of the group. The courses under the combination of positions 2 and 3 made more provision for this element than the other courses, showed more frequent statements of a guiding point of view, and more apparent relationship between their professed philosophy and their suggested experiences.

XIII. ACQUAINTANCE WITH THE NATIONAL CULTURE FOR APPRECIATION AND IMPROVEMENT

As Characterized in the "Guide for the Evaluation of Elementary Curricula" and Found through Its Use

Does this course provide opportunity for the examination (increasingly critical with growing maturity) of the national culture, through:

A. Provision for numerous experiences, which acquaint the child

with our national culture, build an attitude of intelligent appreciation of its most constructive elements, and as he grows older
develop an increasing ability to see and weigh and judge aspects
which seem less constructive?

B. Recognition of the problems of the early Americans in shaping
a new government and in maintaining the principles of religious
liberty? Recognition of the national heritage from the various
racial groups in America and their contributions to literature,
science, and industrial development?

C. The utilization of controversial questions, *appropriate for that
age level,* to acquaint the learner with institutions and conditions
as they exist, to encourage an attitude of critical inquiry, and
to develop a technique for open-minded, logical discussion of vital
problems?

Positions which this course may reflect on "Acquaintance with
the National Culture for Appreciation and Improvement."

1. Little provision for acquaintance with the national culture
as such.

2. Some provision inherent in the suggested experiences but little
emphasis given to their use for interpreting and judging the
national culture.

3. Many experiences provided and suggestions given for their
use in relation to judging and appreciating the national culture.

Positions, as defined, for this necessary element in the curriculum
problem through the examination of 71 courses of study:

Position	Number of Courses
1	15
2	40
3	16

Jury judgment agreement with the writer's evaluation of acquaintance
with the national culture . . . 79 per cent.

Running like a red thread throughout the experience-situations
set up under this guiding element is the need for critical thinking.
Intelligent appreciation of the national culture necessitates the
gradual building up of an attitude of critical inquiry rather than
one of blind acceptance. Appreciation of, and loyalty to, the most
constructive aspects are expected. Examination and improvement
of the less constructive elements are continuously necessary. It is

only in this way that fundamental principles can be maintained and re-evaluated above the machinery of the institutions devised to embody them.

The responsibility of the school, together with that of the home, for this guiding element increases in the proportion to which change is taking place in the child's environment. Professor Counts says: "Our social institutions and practices, all of them, should be critically examined." [11:37] The ability to do critical thinking is a great stabilizing influence with possibilities of maximum service during periods of confusion. The foundation for this necessary ability must be laid, largely, through dynamic experiences vital to the learner. Adults, without laboratory knowledge of the experience-situation type of educational program, frequently underestimate the extent to which children of elementary school age can see and weigh and judge—in short, do critical thinking.

The application of this desirable ability to the various elements set up under this guiding element should acquaint the child with something of the national culture. It should help him appreciate its most constructive aspects, build an attitude toward improving the less constructive ones, lead him to expect change, and develop further ability to do critical thinking. On the need for developing in the child the attitude and ability to think through problems, appropriate to his age level, Professor Kilpatrick writes as follows:

Encourage in the growing child such an appropriate study of our changing world as would help him to grow in the power and disposition to think independently of tradition or prejudice about matters of social and public interest. [38:182]

UNDERLYING ASPECTS ON WHICH THESE FINDINGS WERE
COLLECTED

There is inherent in the history of the development of this country much gripping material for building an attitude of appreciation in the minds of growing children toward the national culture. Some acquaintance with the culture for this purpose is important. The hardships of the early colonists in gaining a foothold in the New World may give the cause for which many of them came an added emphasis. The struggles of the colonies to establish and maintain a government based upon the principles to which they had pledged their goods, lives, and sacred honor are freighted with interest to the youthful learner. The courage and endurance of the pioneer in conquering the physical barriers of the continent, the struggle to preserve the union, the undreamed of advance in the field of science and invention, contributions to literature, and some progress in handling social problems, all have contributed to the national culture and offer interesting experiences for the present-day learner.

The right type of appreciation involves continuous examination to help maintain the principles upon which the national culture is based, and to contribute toward its improvement. This involves critical thinking. It is important to lay the foundation for building an attitude of appreciation of the most constructive elements in the national culture. It is important to awaken an interest as a necessary element in a growing ability to weigh and judge aspects which seem less constructive. Since the national group is composed of many racial groups, the recognition of their various contributions is important to a thorough understanding of the national culture. In acquainting the learner with conditions and institutions as they exist today, controversial questions, suitable for *that age level*, should be used. Such experiences should encourage a wholesome attitude of critical inquiry and provide many opportunities to begin the development of the ability to discuss vital problems in an open-minded and logical manner.

These basic elements, together with the positions previously defined, have served as guiding lines for collecting these findings.

DISCUSSION OF THE FINDINGS FOR "ACQUAINTANCE WITH THE NATIONAL CULTURE FOR APPRECIATION AND IMPROVEMENT"

Position 1

Little provision for acquaintance with the national culture, as such . . . 21 per cent (approximately) of the 71 courses examined. These conditions were found:

	Courses
Total number of courses under Position 1	15
Courses in which the materials were estimated as wholly under this position	15
Courses which stated a guiding point of view, used subject matter objectives, and showed little or no application of their professed philosophy to their suggested experiences	3

Courses which used subject matter objectives only 12
Courses in which the material was estimated under the most
    formal position set up for subject matter 14

Distribution by subjects of the courses in this group: general courses — 2; social studies — 0; art — 1; arithmetic — 12. These courses showed little provision for acquaintance with the national culture. They were among those which made little or no provision for the choice of curriculum experiences on the part of the learner or for creative experiences.

Position 2

Some provision inherent in the suggested experiences but little emphasis given to their use for interpreting and judging the national culture . . . 56 per cent (approximately) of the 71 courses examined.

These conditions were found:

	Courses
Total number of courses under Position 2	40
Courses which showed suggested experiences in which this guiding element was inherent but little emphasis was given to its use	40
Courses which expressed their philosophy through subject matter objectives	16
Courses which stated a guiding philosophy for the curriculum as a whole and used specific objectives as well	24
Courses, of the latter group, which showed a consistent effort to apply their professed philosophy to the suggested experiences	20
Courses in which the materials showed the full range of the positions set up under subject matter with the major portion estimated in the two least formal ones	40

Distribution by subjects of the courses under this position: general courses — 10; social studies — 13; art — 13; arithmetic — 4. It is interesting to compare the number of social studies, art, and arithmetic courses under this position with those under position 1. The findings under this position further emphasized a situation found for other guiding elements. Suggested curriculum experiences showed inherent provision for the elements embodied in this criterion, but their use to this purpose was not emphasized to interpret and judge the national culture. This should be noted as important by persons guiding subsequent curriculum experiences. Its implications are twofold. First, it is important to lead the child to appreciate the constructive elements in his national culture and to begin to build an attitude toward the intelligent examination and improvement of it. Second, it is vital to provide experiences for critical thinking.

Position 3

Many experiences provided and suggestions given for their use in relation to judging and appreciating the national culture . . . 22 per cent (approximately) of the 71 courses examined.

These conditions were found:

	Courses
Total number of courses under Position 3	16
Courses which showed suggested experiences embodying the elements set up under this position	16
Courses which emphasized, to varying extent, the use of these experiences for the purpose designated	11
Courses which stated a guiding point of view for the whole problem and specific objectives as well	16
Courses which showed a consistent effort to apply their professed philosophy to the suggested experiences	14
Courses which stated an attitude on the need for an acquaintance with the national culture	10
Courses which had their materials estimated wholly within the two most informal positions set up for subject matter	16

Distribution by subjects of the 16 courses under this position: general courses — 5; social studies — 9; art — 2; arithmetic — o. As the provision for acquaintance with the national culture for its appreciation and improvement increased, the estimated position of the materials under subject matter moved from the most formal toward the most informal position.

A wide range of suggested experiences to acquaint the child with the national culture appeared in the materials in this group of courses. Community history, holidays, state and national history, customs, great leaders, literature, and current events were all utilized to reflect the heritage. One course prefaced a study of "Pioneer Days," in that particular city, with:

Any local past properly realized, not only contributes in a general way to a feeling of reality in dealing with the larger past, but supplies specific elements for reconstructing the larger past. [34:203]

Another course provided for improvement in the national culture through developing: "the disposition to question current customs constructively." [75:3]

It is an important contribution to the educative process of the child to begin the building of an attitude of appreciation for his national heritage and to help develop the ability to continuously examine and improve it. Here lies an area freighted with rich opportunities for critical thinking. Life presents increasingly numerous and challenging problems. Critical thinking is required. Education that functions must capitalize all possible opportunities to develop this ability. Of the necessity for examining our traditions by means of careful, critical thinking Bode says:

All education . . . should help to create a sense that our traditions require reconstruction and thus provide community of understandings and interests, regardless of its content. In so doing it widens the area of common purposes by weakening the antagonisms that spring from complacent short-sightedness and from stupid loyalties to the past. Real education humanizes men. It does so, however, not by moulding them into unthinking acceptance of pre-established patterns, but by stimulating them to a continuous reconstruction of their outlook on life. [3:31]

SUMMARY

The findings under the three positions set up for this guiding element show an early stage of an interesting movement which should make a definite contribution to our national life. Under positions 1 and 2 there appeared 77 per cent of all the materials examined. These courses either made little provision for acquaintance with the national culture or gave little emphasis to the use of any inherent possibilities to this end. Such a condition reflects the loss of many opportunities for practice in critical thinking. Approximately 22 per cent of the materials appeared under position 3, which provided many experiences and emphasized their use. These facts indicate that attention is beginning to be centered upon an aspect of the curriculum problem which gives promise of making a contribution to our national life through the appreciation of its culture and the critical thinking necessary to improve it. As possibilities for acquaintance with the national culture seemed to increase, the estimated position under content moved from the most formal toward the most informal position. The courses which made the most provision for the elements under consideration showed the most consistent relationship between their professed philosophy and the suggested experiences.

Intelligent appreciation of the national culture necessitates the gradual building up of an attitude of critical inquiry rather than one of blind acceptance. Appreciation of, and loyalty to, the most constructive aspects are expected. Examination and improvement of the less constructive elements are continuously necessary. It is only in this way that fundamental principles can be maintained and re-evaluated above the machinery of the institutions devised to embody them.

XIV. PROVISION FOR GROWTH IN WORLD-MINDEDNESS

As Characterized in the "Guide for the Evaluation of Elementary Curricula" and Found through Its Use

Does this course show provision, in part, for building interest in other national cultures, through:

A. Experiences, *appropriate for the age level,* which acquaint the child with interesting phases of life in other lands; build respect for customs of other peoples; develop an appreciation of their contributions to the arts and sciences; develop an appreciation of the constructive aspects in their national culture; and increase his ability, as he grows older, to see and weigh and judge aspects which seem less constructive?

B. The utilization of the possible contributions of the various racial groups within our own community and the larger national group?

Positions which this course may show on "Provision for Growth in World-Mindedness":

1. Little or no provision for experiences which build international interest.
2. Some provision inherent in the suggested program of experiences, but little evidence of their use in building further interest.
3. A well-balanced program of suggested experiences with many provisions for building further international interest.

Positions, as defined above, found for this increasingly needed element through the examination of 71 courses of study:

Position	Courses
1	21
2	37
3	13

Jury-judgment agreement with the writer's evaluation of "Provision for Growth in World-Mindedness" . . . 84 per cent.

The need for growth in world-mindedness has been pushed ahead, practically overnight, from being an element desired to being an element of great necessity. Among a number of other factors, the comparatively recent gigantic strides in communication and transportation have resulted in quickened relationships all along the international lines and are largely responsible for the present need. Not only are the far-flung sections of the larger countries becoming more closely knit together, but the nations of the world face trade and social contacts for which they must work out new patterns of behavior. That the need for growth in world-mindedness will increase is evident from every quarter of the present picture of world conditions. Trends of today are facts of tomorrow. To meet these facts intelligently the growing individual and his group need as many experiences as possible to gain the necessary information, recognize constructive elements, appreciate the various contributions, and see and weigh less constructive aspects. It is now necessary to build an attitude for dealing with many problems which will increasingly reach across geographical, racial, and so-called political boundaries.

If education is to function to its fullest as a dynamic force in society it faces a real challenge at this point. The opportunities and responsibilities implied in building an attitude of world-mindedness are far-reaching at any time. During a crucial period in world history they become multiplied. That sincere beginnings have been made by different groups, in building better international attitudes should be recognized. Existing conditions and rapidly increasing world contacts force the need for world-mindedness to the fore as a vital educational problem. To have some part in laying the foundation of an attitude to serve this need may well be a privilege and responsibility of the elementary school.

Of the scope of this problem and the possible contribution of education to its solution, Bode says:

We have built up geographical and commercial and linguistic and educational boundaries which inevitably breed crime and war. . . . Wars and crimes are not inevitable because the social environment is not unchangeable. . . . Brilliant triumphs of science have wrought a complete change in our attitude toward the physical. As a consequence we are constantly making over our material surroundings to suit our needs. On the social side our development is still a long way behind. The development is retarded in a large part because of educational practices. When our educational systems become imbued with a humane social ideal our social development will rival our material development and man will no longer be the creature but the master of his environment. [4:243]

UNDERLYING ASPECTS ON WHICH THESE FINDINGS WERE
COLLECTED

Under this guiding element, "Provision for Growth in World-Mindedness," a continuous program of experiences planned to build an interest in the peoples of other lands and to lay the foundation of a friendly attitude toward them stands out. With sensitivity for the selection of experiences appropriate for the age level of the child, the interesting and colorful phases of the life of a national group are studied. Respect for their customs and appreciation of their contributions to the arts and sciences are built up. The most constructive aspects in their national culture are emphasized. As the child grows older he is led to see and weigh the aspects which seem less constructive.

The utilization of the possible contributions of various racial groups, within the community and the national group, may serve a twofold purpose. Here lies an immediate opportunity to acquaint the child with his own national culture and at the same time further build an attitude of respect for similar racial groups outside his own country. The customs, language, songs, and dances of the various groups are especially interesting to children of elementary school age. Such experiences are not only valuable in building constructive attitudes for the American-born child, but they also serve to clothe these contributions with new values for the child of foreign-born parentage. The latter value is frequently overlooked, although it carries a real contribution for the child in this position as he struggles to make his adjustment between two cultures. These major elements, then, and the positions, previously defined, were the guiding lines used to collect these findings.

Position 1
Little or no provision for experiences which build international interest . . . 29 per cent (approximately) of the 71 courses examined.

These conditions were found:

	Courses
Total number of courses under Position 1	21
Courses in which there was practically no provision for experiences planned for building interest in other national cultures	21
Courses which used a statement of a point of view and specific objectives to express their philosophy	5
Courses which used subject matter objectives only under the guiding element dealing with philosophy	16
Courses which showed some application of their professed philosophy to their suggested experiences	4
Courses which had all, or the major portion, of their materials estimated in the most formal position under subject matter	17

Distribution by subjects of the courses in this group: general courses —3; social studies—2; art—3; arithmetic—13. This group of courses showed little or no provision for experiences which build international interest. Their suggested subject matter was largely of the most formal type.

Position 2

Some provision inherent in the suggested program of experiences but little evidence of their use in building further interest . . . 52 per cent (approximately) of the 71 courses examined.

These conditions were found:

	Courses
Total number of courses under Position 2	37
Courses which stated specific objectives only under the guiding element set up for the philosophy	13
Courses which used a statement of a point of view for the total problem and specific objectives to express their philosophy	24
Courses which showed consistency in the application of their guiding point of view to the suggested experiences	18
Courses in this group which had their materials estimated in the full range of positions from the most formal to the most informal one set up for subject matter	37

Distribution by subjects of the courses of this group: general courses —11; social studies—12; art—11; arithmetic—3. The social studies and art courses outnumbered the arithmetic courses.

The findings for this position repeated a condition previously brought out in this study. The elements included in this position were inherent—to some degree—in the curriculum materials but little or no emphasis was given to their use. This group comprised 52 per cent of the courses examined under this guiding element. Most educators will agree that making provision for building interest in other national cultures is a curriculum problem of unusual moment. That this is an area challenging further consideration may well be conceded. This position, then, showed opportunities which were uncapitalized to promote further growth in world-mindedness.

Position 3

A rich, well-balanced program of suggested experiences with many provisions for building further international interest . . . 18 per cent (approximately) of the 71 courses examined.

These conditions were found:

	Courses
Total number of courses under Position 3	13
Courses which showed definite provision for building further international interest	13
Courses which showed statements of a point of view and specific objectives to express their philosophy	13
Courses which showed a consistent effort to apply their professed philosophy to their suggested experiences	12
Courses which had their materials estimated in the two most informal positions set up for subject matter	13

Distribution by subjects of the courses in this group: general courses —2; social studies—9; art—2; arithmetic—0. The predominance of social studies courses is again interesting to note in the group which made the most provision for growth in world-mindedness. Only 18 per cent of the 71 courses examined made definite provision for experiences planned toward building so important an attitude as international interest. This fact may serve as a guide to subsequent curriculum experiences.

This group of courses made provision for the elements set up under position 3. They stated a guiding philosophy for the curriculum as a whole as well as specific subject objectives. They showed a consistent effort to apply this philosophy to all phases of the problem. Their materials were estimated under the most informal positions set up for the guiding element dealing with subject matter. The courses under this position showed the most consistent relationship between their professed philosophy and their suggested educational experiences.

Among many suggested experiences planned for building further international interest, one course in this group showed the following:

> Specific values derived from the experiences involving Swiss life. Knowledge and appreciation of how the Swiss people live. That they maintain no standing army [1931]. [36:209]

Another course lists as suggested experiences:

> [A study of] Ways in which Peoples in Different Parts of the World Help Each Other. . . . Friendly correspondence with children of other countries. [65:36]

Climaxing a study in the fifth and sixth grades of the "Inter-dependence among Nations of the World," a course in this group says:

> Perhaps the greatest gain which grew out of this study was the tolerance the children developed for other people. The fact that we would like to be friends and are interested in knowing more about these peoples . . . will no doubt impress on the children's minds the idea of all nations in the world living together in peace and harmony. [32:46]

SUMMARY

The findings for this guiding element, like those pertaining to the national culture, show the beginnings of a movement. This one promises to build an interest in other national cultures. That this element, outstanding as a world need at present, should be inherent in 52 per cent of the suggested experiences and not capitalized reflects a condition needing further careful study. It seemed evident, under position 3, that 18 per cent of the materials made provision for building interest in other national cultures. Since the courses in this latter group were among those which made the most provision for other guiding elements used in this study, it seemed reasonable to infer that the 18 per cent recorded for this position may well be the beginning of a wider movement for making "Provision for Growth in World-Mindedness."

The need for growth in world-mindedness has advanced from an element desired to a necessity. Trends of today become facts of tomorrow. It is now necessary to build an attitude for dealing with many problems which will increasingly reach across geographical, racial, and so-called political boundaries.

XV. SUBJECT MATTER: HOW THOUGHT OF AND HOW ACCORDINGLY USED

As Characterized in the "Guide for the Evaluation of Elementary Curricula" and Found through Its Use

How does this course conceive of subject matter and how provide for its use?

A. *Subject-matter-set-out-to-be-learned.* This is the common or ordinary traditional position regarding curriculum. It is usually presented in the form of an outline of subject matter determined in advance by adults, chosen for later use, and acquired largely through memorization.

B. *Subject matter largely predetermined, but enlivened by various activities.* In this position subject matter, in the traditional sense, is largely determined in advance by adults, but the introduction of various activities to accomplish this program embodies some choice on the part of learner and some enrichment of content.

C. *Subject matter as a means to an end.* This position considers as subject matter what is found necessary and drawn in to solve a problem, which may or may not have been chosen jointly by the learner and adults.

D. *Subject matter as the total experience.* This position considers subject matter as *all the values* accruing out of participation in the choice of the enterprise, all attendant experiences, enriching materials, and efforts involved in the satisfactory completion of the undertaking.

Positions which this course may reflect on subject matter:

1. Subject-matter-set-out-to-be-learned.
2. Subject matter largely predetermined but enlivened by various activities.
3. Subject matter as a means to an end.
4. Subject matter as the total experience.

Positions, as defined above, found for this central element in the curriculum problem through the examination of 71 courses of study:

Position	Number of Courses
1	12
2	19
3	17
4	23

Jury judgment agreement with the writer's evaluation of "Subject Matter: How Thought of and How Accordingly Used" . . . 92 per cent.

The curriculum maker's concept of subject matter is largely synonymous with his point of view on the curriculum problem as a whole. Here lies one of the high-pressure areas of the nation-wide interest in the curriculum. The answer to the question—What is subject matter?—may well reflect a composite of all the guiding elements, and more, set up for use in this study. From the professed philosophy to the point of view on the acquisition of necessary skills these elements are all embodied in this question. Current curriculum materials reflect the full gamut of opinions from the traditional body of predetermined subject matter to dynamic experience-situations vital to the learner. At one end of the subject matter scale lies a body of fixed, adult-determined material to be learned largely by memorization. At the other end of this subject matter scale lie increasingly rich and changing experiences comprising life itself for the learner. In and through these experiences life is improved, and the personality of the learner may have a fairer chance to grow.

Writing with respect to this important problem a generation ago Dewey says:

Abandon the notion of subject matter as something fixed and ready-made in itself, outside the child's experience. [19:16]

The child is the starting point, the center, and the end. His development, his growth, is the ideal. It alone furnishes the standard. To the growth of the child all studies are subservient; they are instruments valued as they serve the needs of growth. Personality, character, is more than subject matter. No knowledge or information, but self realization, is the goal. To possess all the world of knowledge and lose one's own self is as awful a fate in education as in religion. Moreover, subject matter never can be got into the child from without. Learning is active. It involves reaching out of the mind. It involves organic assimilation starting from within. Literally we must take our stand with the child and our departure from him. It is he not subject matter which determines both quality and quantity of learning. [19:13]

Writing at the present time Professor Kilpatrick emphasizes the relationship between subject matter and life:

As for subject matter—if only we can form guiding conceptions as to how to steer life so that as life it becomes more adequate, subject matter will largely take care of itself. This is not to say that there is no problem of how to conceive and manage this sort of life—the contrary is most acutely true. But it is to say that we do not need to think first of certain supposedly desirable subject matter, whether it shall get learned. Our first and last thought is of life and personality, twin aspects of the same process, that the two may grow jointly in the most defensible way we can manage. If this be well done, more and not less of "subject matter" will be needed and it will be better "learned" than hitherto. [39:23]

UNDERLYING ASPECTS ON WHICH THESE FINDINGS
WERE COLLECTED

The concept of subject-matter-set-out-to-be-learned is deeply intrenched. It has prevailed, largely intact, through much of the period since the beginning of the present century. It carries the implication of being wholly determined in advance by adults, chosen for later use, and acquired by the learner chiefly through memorization. Closely linked to this point of view on subject matter, teaching by separate subjects has been the common practice. In this procedure the logical rather than the psychological organization of subject matter has been stressed. Acquisition of facts recorded through examinations determined the success of the learner. Misapplied phases of the test and measurement movement have tended, in some areas, to help maintain the status quo of the traditional subject matter position. Several major influences have assailed this point of view. It gives way slowly. Even where progress has been made interesting reflections of the subject-matter-set-out-to-be-learned type of suggested experience still persist. These range in type from lists of "Poems to Be Memorized" through the numerous aspects of the "Minimum Essentials." Not infrequently opinion comes to grip in evaluating an entire educational program upon the long over-emphasized need of memorizing a traditional body of number facts, which have been parceled out for consumption at various grade levels. Such a point of view has been embodied under position 1 of this guiding element—*subject-matter-set-out-to-be-learned.*

The traditional position regarding subject matter has been assailed by a number of influences. A generation of the teachings of a philosophy which has based its assumptions upon a biological psychology and emphasized experiencing as a central tenet has made a marked inroad. The unusual advance in many aspects of the child study movement, within the present century, has increasingly centered attention upon the growing individual rather than chiefly upon so-called subject matter. Rapid social and economic changes which reflected the lag between the traditional point of view in the curriculum and life outside the school have steadily pressed upon the situation. These major influences are involved in the nation-wide interest in the curriculum problem. Slow but encouraging progress has been made in the beginnings of a movement to swing the emphasis somewhat away from the traditional point of view. In the early stages of these influences interesting results were reflected in the curriculum materials. Some of these results are embodied under position 2, *subject matter largely predetermined, but enlivened by various activities.* Here subject matter is largely determined in advance by adults. The influence of a philosophy which has long emphasized experiencing is reflected in the activities haltingly introduced. These "activities" afforded some enrichment of the curriculum experiences and provided some choice on the part of the learner.

With the introduction of the point of view that real learning was most likely to take place through the solution of a problem, the definition of subject matter went through another stage in its growth. Position 3, *subject matter as a means to an end,* has been set up to embody this point of view in the early stages of its reflection in the curriculum materials. This position considers as subject matter what is found necessary and drawn in to solve a problem, which may, or may not, have been chosen jointly by the learner and adults.

As the influences, previously discussed, are becoming more effective subject matter is beginning to take on a richer, more inclusive concept. Position 4, *subject matter as the total experience,* has been set up to embody this stage in its growth. This position considers subject matter as *all the values* accruing out of participation in the choice of the enterprise, all attendant experiences, enriching materials, information gained, new areas disclosed for further exploration, skills recognized by the learner as necessary and acquired to meet a need, and the efforts involved in the satisfactory completion and enjoyment of the undertaking. This position involves life for the learner.

There is no assumption that these four positions adequately cover all stages of the changing concept of subject matter. However, it is maintained that they do furnish thinking points to aid in portraying the range from the traditional formal type to the dynamic concept of subject matter, which is involved in the total experience. There seems to be little evidence that any one of these positions represents a universally accepted point of view at any given period, although one type may be more dominant while reshaping forces are at work in the process of continuous change. That several points of view exist simultaneously should be capitalized as a valuable opportunity for critical thinking. For the writer the concept of *subject matter as the total experience* seems most conducive to growth.

Position 1

Subject-matter-set-out-to-be-learned . . . 17 per cent (approximately) of the 71 courses examined.

These conditions were found:

	Courses
Total number of courses under Position 1	12
Courses in which the major portion of the materials appeared wholly under this most formal position	12
Courses in which the core of the materials embodied so-called "Minimum Essentials"	10
Courses which showed subject matter objectives under the guiding element dealing with the philosophy	12
Courses which made no statement of a point of view for the curriculum as a whole	12

Distribution by subjects of the courses under this position: general courses—2; social studies—0; art—0; arithmetic—10. The same condition is reflected here as appeared under the most formal positions set up for the other guiding elements. Social studies and art courses either do not appear at all or are present in very small numbers compared to the arithmetic courses. There was little or no provision in these courses for learning through first-hand experiences, the utilization or enrichment of the environment, choice on the part of the learner, provision for creative experience, or growth in intellectual curiosity. Since there was no guiding point of view expressed, the question of the relationship between the philosophy and the suggested experiences was not involved.

Position 2

Subject matter largely predetermined, but enlivened by various activities . . . 27 per cent (approximately) of the 71 courses examined.

These conditions were found:

	Courses
Total number of courses under Position 2	19
Courses which recorded the introduction of various activities to help "put over" a body of subject matter chosen in advance by adults	19
Courses in which there was little indication that these activities were introduced for their own possible contribution to child growth	19
Courses which used a guiding point of view and subject matter objectives under the guiding element concerned with the philosophy	8
Courses, of the latter group, which attempted to apply their guiding point of view through the activities suggested to enliven predetermined subject matter	3
Courses which used subject matter objectives only	11

Distribution by subjects of the courses in this group: general courses —5; social studies—6; art—4; arithmetic—4. These courses showed the type of curriculum materials resulting from the influences which questioned the inherited body of subject matter and tried to enrich it. Increasingly rich lists of "Suggested Activities" appeared to enliven predetermined subject matter. This advance enriched the curriculum to some extent and provided a measure of opportunity for choice on the part of the learner.

Position 3

Subject matter as a means to an end . . . 24 per cent (approximately) of the 71 courses examined.

These conditions were found:

	Courses
Total number of courses under Position 3	17
Courses in which the materials reflected the point of view that so-called subject matter was what was necessary to solve some problem	17

Courses which used both a statement of a guiding point of view and subject matter objectives to express their philosophy   13
Courses which showed some evidence that effort had been made to apply the guiding philosophy to the suggested experiences   13
Courses which used subject matter objectives only   4

Distribution by subjects of the courses estimated under this position: general courses—2; social studies—7; art—7; arithmetic—1. As the number of social studies, art, and less formal general courses increased, the provision for the experience-situation type of curriculum material became more apparent. These courses showed increased opportunity for choice of the curriculum activities on the part of the learner. They showed more first-hand experiences, more provision for experience-situations, and more opportunity for creative experience. The inter-relationship between the professed philosophy and the suggested experiences was evident.

Position 4

Subject matter as the total experience . . . 32 per cent (approximately) of the 71 courses examined.

These conditions were found:

	Courses
Total number of courses under Position 4	23
Courses in which the major portion of the materials appeared under this position	23
Courses which varied regarding the inclusiveness of subject matter as the total experience but showed an advance in considering more of the elements of an experience-situation as the so-called subject matter	23
Courses which used a guiding point of view and subject matter objectives to express their philosophy	23

Distribution by subjects of the courses under this position: general courses—8; social studies—9; art—4; arithmetic—2. From position 1 through position 4 the number of social studies courses have increased. This group of courses offered more opportunity for choice of the curriculum experiences on the part of the learner than any group set up for subject matter. They made provision for the utilization and enrichment of the environment, many first-hand experiences, creative experience, and the encouragement of intellectual curiosity.

On this pivotal element, "Subject Matter: How Thought of and How Accordingly Used," in the curriculum problem one course in the group under position 4 expresses its point of view as follows:

Our point of view is that the curriculum is a series of experiences concerned with any growing out of things of real interest to the child. . . . We are teaching children, not subject matter, and we teach subject matter as children have need of it in a natural situation. Subject matter can never be gotten into the child from without. Learning is active. The child learns by doing. [60:22]

Subject matter divisions should be disregarded in the study of problems of wide social significance. [60:14]

This course showed many suggested experience-situations in which this point of view was consistently applied.

Another course, under position 4, which consistently reflected an awareness of child growth and which considered subject matter as the total experience, affirms: ". . . Their own [the children's] experiences furnish the best subject matter." [1:14] This same course showed an outstanding relationship between the guiding philosophy used and the suggested experience-situations. It further declared a point of view as follows:

We believe that these experiences integrate subject matter and eliminate sharply drawn distinctions between the conventional school subjects. [1:iv]

With respect to the child's total experience, this course further states:

Due to the influence of Dewey, Kilpatrick, McMurry, and others attention has more and more been centered upon the child's reaction to all that is placed before him, curricular and otherwise. [1:i]

Even a partial realization of subject matter as the total experience may be expected to be a long, slow process. Its importance to the fullest development of the individual is increasingly emphasized by advanced thinkers in the field. Our inherited concept of compartmentalized subjects and their values gives way slowly. However, progress has been made. Of this tendency Bode says:

Our practice of compartmentalizing different values, both in school and out, has not merely fostered the habit of thinking in terms of fixed patterns, but has provided inhibitions, in case there is any tendency to depart from these patterns. [3:7]

SUMMARY

The findings under these four positions show how slowly the traditional point of view, and its inherited concepts, gives way in response to more recent influences. Positions 1 and 2 show that 40 per cent of the so-called subject matter was definitely predetermined. Under position 3 these findings show that 24 per cent of the materials examined provided the experience-situation type of curriculum content, although many of the attendant values were not considered as subject matter. Proponents of the point of view represented under position 4 may note with satisfaction that 32 per cent is the largest amount of material estimated under any of the positions set up for subject matter. However, the reader is asked to keep in mind the relationship of this segment to the total situation. It is also necessary to recall the fact that this position represents progress toward subject matter as the total experience rather than a record of the accomplishment of any stage of growth. It is here conceived as an aspect in the onward movement of enriching life and building personality.

The curriculum maker's concept of subject matter was largely synonymous with his point of view on the curriculum problem as a whole. As the so-called subject matter progressed from the traditional, predetermined type toward the total experience, statements of a point of view to guide the curriculum as a whole appeared more frequently. In the courses which considered subject matter as the total experience there was more inter-relationship between the professed philosophy and the suggested educational experience.

XVI. THE PLACE OF DRILL

As Characterized in the "Guide for the Evaluation of Elementary Curricula" and Found through Its Use

Does this course show provision for:

A. No drill—no mention of any provision for drill?
B. Disassociated drill—material outlined to be memorized in advance?
C. Associated drill—material experienced as it functions with *the need for drill recognized* both by teacher and learner, and practiced to meet this need?

D. The need for extra drill reduced—material experienced in a rich, well-integrated program providing many opportunities for building associations in learning, and found by pupils and teacher to reduce the need for extra drill?

Positions which this course may show on "The Place of Drill."

1. No mention of drill.
2. Disassociated drill.
3. Associated drill.
4. The need for extra drill reduced.

Positions, as defined above, found for this frequently misunderstood element, drill, through the examination of 71 courses of study:

Position	Number of Courses
1	9
2	16
3	46
4 (small sections of 14 courses listed under Position 3)	

Perhaps no single aspect of the curriculum problem has drawn such heated and prolonged controversy as the one under discussion in this section. The amount of drill outlined in a course of study, was, for a long period, the sign and seal of the excellent curriculum. Investigation has sought the kind of drill which would be most effective in getting certain bodies of facts learned. The laws of learning have exerted a wide influence. The tests and measurement movement has shown its effect. As curricula of certain types have built up their own particular methods, so the type and quantity of drill have been determined to serve these points of view. The curriculum maker's concept of drill is largely synonymous with his concept of subject matter, his concept of how learning takes place, and his acquaintance with the contributions from the fields of psychology and mental hygiene.

At one end of the scale the traditional point of view had certain bodies of subject matter to pour into the mind of the child. To be sure this was done, much drill was necessary. The wrong use of tests frequently entered here. Drill for a supposedly future use went on ad infinitum. At the other end of the scale the influence of a biological psychology, basing learning upon experiencing, reveals to the learner the need for a necessary skill. The opportunity is provided for him to recognize his lack of that particular skill as blocking his pursuit of some problem meaningful to him. This provision builds the association of the need close to the practice necessary to acquire the skill in question. Meeting drill as it functions holds much promise for more effective learning. Here it is made to serve interest and thus escapes the frequently used subterfuge of having to make drill interesting. As Dewey points out: "When things have to be *made* interesting it is because interest itself is wanting." [22:427]

Valuable contributions have been made to the field of drill. Mental hygiene increasingly offers its guidance for the consideration of the concomitant results of drill. These results are often of equal or more importance than the element with which the drill is concerned.

UNDERLYING ASPECTS ON WHICH THESE FINDINGS WERE COLLECTED

In setting up this guiding element, it was intended to represent the full range of opinion from the apparent failure in the curriculum materials to recognize the need for drill over into the point of view that enriched and deepened meanings carry the possibilities of reducing the need for drill. Under position 1 drill has apparently received little or no recognition. The materials showed no mention of this element. Under position 2, disassociated drill, the highly traditional point of view has been set up. Materials are outlined to be memorized in advance of their need. In position 3, associated drill, the need is recognized by the learner through experiencing the materials as they function. This need and the practice to acquire the necessary skill are closely related.

It is the conviction of the writer that the need for extra drill is reduced where the materials are met in a program of dynamic experiences providing many opportunities for building associations in learning. Such a situation has been set up under position 4. When this was done there was no expectation that the materials of any course would be wholly of this type or that all need for drill would be eliminated. However, portions of the materials appearing under.other positions, and especially under position 3, were reasonably expected to reflect this point of view. Investigation on this aspect of drill should make a contribution. These major underlying elements have been used as guiding lines to collect the findings for this important aspect of the curriculum problem.

Position 1

No mention of drill . . . 13 per cent (approximately) of the 71 courses examined.

These conditions were found:

	Courses
Total number of courses under Position 1	9
Courses which made no provision for drill	9
Courses which stated a guiding point of view and subject matter objectives to express their philosophy	7
Courses which stated subject matter objectives only	2
Courses which had their materials estimated from a comparatively middle position toward the most informal one set up for subject matter	9

Distribution by subjects of the courses which made no mention of any provision for drill: general courses—2; social studies—7; art —o; arithmetic—o. These courses, which made no mention of any provision for drill, were drawn from the general and social studies groups. No mention of drill does not imply that drill did not exist, to some degree, as it was necessitated by the various experiences involved in carrying on problems of interest to the group. It is also reasonable to believe that there was growth in the various skills practiced in situations meaningful to the learner. That drill was not mentioned may have been due to the fact that many persons participating in the curriculum problem still hold the concept of disassociated drill, so that they think of drill in connection with other subjects than social studies, the one composing the major portion of this group. They do not recognize the need for capitalizing all meaningful situations requiring further skill to carry on a chosen problem, as the psychological time and place for the drill which is required to gain, or increase, that needed skill.

Position 2

Disassociated drill, 22 per cent (approximately) of the 71 courses examined.

These conditions were found:

	Courses
Total number of courses under Position 2	16
Courses which made provision for drill by outlining it to be memorized in advance of the learner's need for its use	16
Courses which used subject matter objectives under the guiding element dealing with the philosophy	14
Courses which stated a point of view for the total problem as well as subject matter objectives	2
Courses which appeared in the most formal position	12

Distribution by subjects of the courses of this group: general courses —4; social studies—1; art—1; arithmetic—10. The majority of these courses were among the group which showed little or no provision for the choice of the curriculum experiences on the part of the learner, no provision for creative experience, and used the traditional point of view regarding subject matter. One course in this group states that "The problem of teaching pupils the list of arithmetical facts . . . is mainly one of applying methods which lead to quick and secure memorization." [18:13] Another course holds that: "The necessity of systematic drill, in order that automatic memory results can be had and permanently maintained, cannot be over emphasized." [28:115]

Position 3

Associated drill . . . 64 per cent (approximately) of the 71 courses examined.

These conditions were found:

	Courses
Total number of courses under Position 3	46
Courses in which the materials showed drill associated with the need, recognized by pupils and teacher as necessary, and practiced to that end	46
Courses which used both a statement of a guiding point of view and specific objectives to express their philosophy	32
Courses which used subject matter objectives	14

Distribution by subjects of the courses of this group: general courses —9; social studies—17; art—13; arithmetic—7. As provision for associated drill increased, the number of social studies, art, and general courses of the less formal type appeared in the group. These courses showed many opportunities capitalized from the experience-situations to acquire or increase a skill through its association with a meaningful experience and the necessary drill to meet this need. In a number of the courses this provision for drill was an element in a broader provision for growth which emphasized child development rather than subject matter acquisition. Learning was a process affecting the human organism in its total experience.

Many of the courses in this group were among those which made provision for some choice of the curriculum experiences on the part of the teacher-pupil group, for learning through first-hand experiences, for many opportunities for creative experience, and showed their concept of subject matter, largely, as the total experience. Such a point of view promises optimum growth for the child.

On the important subject of drill associated with the need, one art course in this group says: "When the child asks for help he has reached the need for definite instruction in technique." [25:5] An arithmetic course says: "Teachers and pupils should always feel the purpose of drill. Drill should be based on children's errors and take place when they are ready for it." [64:5] One of the general courses of the special group included in this study says: "All drill should be based on the demonstrated needs of the child." [60:53] Of acquiring a skill Professor Mossman says: "Need it; learn it; use it: this seems to be the order which makes it a part of the learner's living." [47:176]

Position 4

The need for extra drill reduced. None of the 71 courses appeared wholly under this position. Portions of the courses, under position 3, which made the most outstanding provision for the experience-situation type of curricula, reflected the elements defined for position 4 and might well have been discussed here. This position was set up to represent the opposite point of view from that embodied in position 2, or the failure to recognize the need for drill as set up for position 1. It was not expected that entire courses would appear in this position. The question of what constitutes intelligent drill invites much careful investigation. It seems reasonable to believe that the need for extra drill can be reduced when the element in question is experienced in many situations rich in meanings to the child, and practice given to acquire the skill in close association to the need.

SUMMARY

The findings for this guiding element, under position 3, show that the point of view on drill, as recorded in printed curricula, is moving in an encouraging direction. This fact is evident, however tenaciously some of the classroom procedure may cling to the traditional variety. Positions 1 and 2 show 35 per cent of the materials in which drill received no provision, or was of the traditional, disassociated type. This fact regarding the acquisition of necessary skills, important to the child's increasing independence for further investigation, should concern subsequent curriculum efforts.

The curriculum maker's point of view on this question is largely synonymous with his concept of subject matter, how learning takes place, the place of the teacher, pupil-teacher choice of curriculum experience, and his acquaintance with the contributions from the fields of psychology and mental hygiene. There is much promise in the growing emphasis upon the learner's recognition of the need for a skill, and the close association of this need with the practice necessary to acquire that particular skill. This point of view generally insures the use of tests as instruments of instruction recognized as helpful by the teacher and pupils. Experiencing drill as it functions in the acquisition of a necessary skill shows progress made for this aspect of the curriculum problem.

XVII. THE FORM USED IN ORGANIZING THE CURRICULUM MATERIAL

As Characterized in the "Guide for the Evaluation of Elementary Curricula" and Found through Its Use

What form is used in this course?

A. *A bare topical outline* of "subject-matter-set-out-to-be-learned."
   No suggestions are given for enriching materials, related activities, or choice of experiences on the part of the learner.

B. *An outline, somewhat enriched, of subject matter to be covered.*
   Suggestions are given for enriching materials and related activities involving some choice on the part of the learner.

C. *An elective list of suggested activities within certain subject matter areas.* Freedom in the choice is emphasized. Much help is given on related activities and enriching materials. A record of the organization, procedure, and materials used in working out a problem is offered for guidance of the teacher.

D. *An integrated program of experiences.* Using large objectives to promote range and balance, a rich, integrated program of experience-situations is suggested. Provision is made for the learner to share in the suggestions and choice of the enterprise, to work toward ends agreed upon jointly by the teacher and the learners, to participate in all attendant experiences, and the evaluation of results growing out of the satisfactory completion of the chosen undertaking. (The integrated program may or may not appear as Units of Work.)

E. *Units of Work.*
   a. A program of experiences integrated to some degree, but reflecting elements of standardization.
   b. A rich, well-integrated experience of social significance to the child.

F. A statement recommending that the curriculum be "made as you go."
   a. No guiding criteria given.
   b. Educational aims given for guidance.

Positions which this course may show on the form used for the curriculum materials:

1. A bare topical outline.
2. An outline, somewhat enriched, of subject matter to be covered.
3. An elective list of suggested activities within certain subject matter areas.
4. An integrated program of experiences.
5. Units of Work.
6. A statement recommending that the curriculum be "made as you go."

Positions, as defined above, used for the organization of curriculum material and found through the examination of 71 courses:

Position	Number of Courses
1	6
2	20
3	7
4	15
5	23
6	0

Jury judgment agreement with the writer's evaluation of "The Form Used in Organizing the Curriculum Material" . . . 96 per cent.

The reader is here requested to consider "form," in its application to the organization of curriculum materials, not merely as such but for the deeper implications which it carries. It is this latter aspect that has determined its inclusion in this study.

As certain types of curriculum experiences have gradually built up the methods which seem best to serve that point of view, so the form used in organizing the curriculum materials reflects its point of view. Some consideration of this element largely reveals the curriculum maker's concept of subject matter, his theory of the way learning takes place, his knowledge of child development as a whole, and his educational philosophy—in short his curriculum thinking.

The bare topical outline, of position 1, is quite adequate to set forth the traditional, predetermined curriculum material of the subject-matter-set-out-to-be-learned type. Position 2 moves a step ahead. It offers an outline of subject matter to be covered with some enriching materials and related activities. There is some small amount of choice on the part of the learner. Another step ahead is set up, under position 3, with an elective list of "suggested activities" within certain subject matter areas. Freedom in choice is involved. The teacher-pupil group is given guidance on their chosen problem through records of the organization, procedure, and materials used in working out other problems. Under position 4, an integrated program of experiences is provided. This form used large objectives to promote range and balance. A rich program of experience-situations is suggested. This provides much opportunity for choice of and responsibility for the curriculum experiences on the part of the learner. Such a program may or may not appear as "Units of Work." Under position 5, Units of Work frequently are of two types. In one, the experiences are integrated to some degree, but show the grip of standardization. In the other, experiences vital to the child center about the solution of the problem in hand with the total experience recognized as subject matter. Under position 6, recommending that the curriculum be "made as you go," two types appear—one in which no guiding criteria is given, the other using educational aims for guidance.

From the bare topical outline throughout all the forms of organization here used, there are implications which carry meanings important to the curriculum problem.

SUMMARY

The findings for this element of the curriculum problem show a distinct trend away from the bare topical outline as defined for position 1. It is interesting to note the large per cent of the materials that appeared under position 2 in which predetermined subject matter still holds forth although somewhat enlivened by activities which provide some choice on the part of the learner. Positions 4 and 5 showed 38 per cent of the materials examined and both emphasized an advance toward a well-integrated program of experience. These courses showed more first-hand experiences, more choice on the part of the learner, and more provision for creative experience. They reflected more concern for the all-round development of the child. As provision for these elements and others embodied in the guide increased, statements of a guiding point of view for the problem as a whole became more frequent. The inter-relationship between the professed philosophy and the suggested experiences to carry out this philosophy appeared more consistently.

XVIII. SOME INCONSISTENCIES BETWEEN THE
PHILOSOPHY AND THE SUGGESTED EXPERIENCES

As Characterized in the "Guide for the Evaluation of Elementary Curricula" and Found through Its Use

Outstanding Inconsistencies in this course between the *Philosophy* and the *Suggested Experiences*: The examiners were asked to record illustrations, using quotations and giving references, under the headings "Philosophy" and "Suggested Experiences."

The application of this inquiry to the curriculum materials in the 71 courses examined resulted in an interesting body of findings. The most outstanding inconsistencies were emphasized owing to the fact that a field of such breadth required some limiting element. These inconsistencies appeared in a wide range as to type and estimated extent. They were apparent in courses in which any stated guiding point of view for the problem as a whole was an isolated matter, with little or no evidence of its application to the suggested experiences. At the opposite end of a possible scale for curriculum materials some slight inconsistencies frequently appeared. This was true even in courses which had made provision for the various guiding elements used, and showed evidence of the application of their professed philosophy to the suggested experiences.

The inconsistencies discussed here will be representative of a large number of cases. They stand out as the type which most frequently reflects the failure to arrive at and explicitly state a guiding philosophy for curriculum making and the consistent application of this philosophy to the suggested educational experiences. These cases will be drawn from two areas. Those relating to the curriculum problem as a whole will be emphasized. Those dealing more directly with subject matter will be included to focus attention upon the conflicts that are reflected between so-called specific objectives and the suggested experiences to carry out their point of view.

Case 1

From the Guiding Point of View Stated. One course records: "Dr. Dewey of Columbia says, regarding the way in which we deal with children, 'Wise guidance is not eternal imposition, but the freeing of power for future use.'" [69:15]

From the Suggested Experiences. The same course quoted above showed the entire kindergarten curriculum outlined by weeks. From September to June this predetermined weekly plan for the central activity, or short-timed central interest, ran its course.

There is no question that many of the suggestions in the outline just mentioned carry value. When put into action these suggestions, no doubt, stimulate other interests. For that type of curriculum experience they may be well interpreted. However, if the learner is to have his full powers freed and developed—as embodied in the chosen guiding point of view quoted—every opportunity to this end should be capitalized. A course of study definitely outlined by weeks offers the minimum opportunity for planning and choice on the part of the learner. Such a program fails to recognize the vital grip of interest necessitating that the element of the time spent upon an activity should be determined by a teacher-pupil decision. In studying the child's total experience in such a situation, the examiner is forced to regret the loss of those dynamic values which are possible only through acquaintance with the immediate interests of the individual and his group, and provision of opportunities which embody planning, choosing, achieving, sharing, and enjoying results. It is only upon this sound psychological basis that a new experience can become integrated with the child's past experience through the building of new meanings. Such elements help to enrich and extend the child's interests. It is maintained that the concept of curriculum experiences recorded under case 1 largely limits rather than liberates the full powers of the child for further growth. Such a condition would indicate that the central tenet of the philosophy quoted had been missed.

Case 2

From the Guiding Point of View. One course recorded in the Foreword the following statement: "The value of a course of study lies in its helpfulness and suggestiveness as a guide to the teachers. In so far as it limits the thoughtful teacher it is faulty; in so far as it aids the work and gives ample latitude to the strong, it is helpful and necessary." [2:1]

From the Suggested Experiences. As a preface to the suggested experiences in the course just quoted the following was recorded: "The teacher's daily program should be conspicuously posted in the classroom and rigidly followed." Also, "It is the duty of each teacher to test the pupils' knowledge of the work required in preceding grades." [2:3]

It is not here intended to imply that the total point of view of this course is represented by the quotations used. However, it is maintained that a distinct conflict exists in a very fundamental aspect of the curriculum problem. The place of the teacher is increasingly important. The quality of the educational program is largely determined by the work of "the thoughtful teacher." Rich experiencing for children takes place only where "ample latitude to the strong" is made possible. These two statements, just quoted, when embodied in all aspects of the curriculum, are offered as a part of the test of a valuable course of study. This point of view is in direct conflict with the order quoted later under case 2 that the "daily program should be conspicuously posted . . . and rigidly followed." Here traditional subject-matter-set-out-to-be-learned is implied. A testing program insured its efficient consumption. Any question as to its value was not reflected.

If the inconsistency which exists here were removed so that ample latitude was truly given to the thoughtful, strong teacher, regulations concerning "rigidly followed" programs would speedily disappear. Ample latitude for the strong teacher implies teacher-pupil choice of the curriculum experiences, within guiding lines: planning, participation, responsibility for decisions, and enjoyment of achievement. It is impossible for even a strong teacher to be limited by such regulations as following an elementary school program rigidly and be able to capitalize or guide immediate, dynamic experiences toward their fullest contribution to the child's total educative process. The teacher-pupil relationship is the most vital one in the school's contribution. The quoted guiding point of view, providing "ample latitude to thoughtful, strong teachers" as a test for a good course of study, is too vital to rich experiences for the child to fail to apply it to the subsequent curriculum content.

Case 3

From the Guiding Point of View. One course recorded the following quotation from Dewey as an expression of their guiding point of view: "The measure of the worth of the curriculum and of the methods of instruction in the school is the extent to which they are animated by the social." [31:5]

From the Suggested Experiences. This guiding philosophy for the curriculum as a whole was followed by a number of excellent subject matter aims in the fields of language, reading, and literature. Some worth-while suggested experiences in each field were recorded. However, the point of view, expressed in the philosophy chosen, was not consistently applied to all the inherent elements. The concept of "social" here quoted involves emphasis upon practice in social living through participation, pupil-teacher choice of the curriculum experiences, and group sharing. This concept implies many in and out of school experiences and meaningful opportunities for membership in the community group.

Case 4

From the Guiding Point of View. In an art course the following point of view is recorded to guide the suggested experiences: "The teacher's part is to guide the pupils in expressing themselves, not to impose adult standards upon them." [54:5] A further element in their point of view is recorded: "The aim of the work in construction is twofold: to develop mechanical skill and to foster creative ability. The first lessons must be carefully planned by the teacher and dictated step by step, but as soon as the mechanical processes have been mastered, the pupil should invent his own means of arriving at the desired end." [54:8]

From the Suggested Experiences. The elements quoted, in the preceding point of view, are followed by an outline of suggested experiences which is largely dictated and is not the outgrowth of the child's experience. The following body of suggestions reflect a fundamental inconsistency: "In preparation for project work, draw the following—" [54:90] In this case there appeared a conflict within the point of view. Free expression of an idea by the child, over against highly dictated drill experience disassociated from its need, stands out. If the guiding point of view, first quoted for this case, is consistently applied techniques will be developed out of actual experience. It will then follow that the art experiences will grow out of a need for their contribution to help convey some idea involved in the "project work" and because of this need become vital to the child's total experience. The procedure reflected in the second quotation regarding the development of technique is contrary to the best current opinion in which a skill is closely associated with its need, and the practice to acquire it is given or started at that time.

Case 5

From the Guiding Point of View. Typical of a number of courses in this field is one which records, as an aspect of its "aims," "To re-establish the fact that arithmetic is necessary to life during vacation as well as during school time. To maintain and develop skills which have been established." [46:1]

From the Suggested Experiences. The course just quoted showed suggested experiences to meet the formal element of its aims, but recorded little provision for experiences to capitalize vital number situations in the child's environment, or to extend his number horizon. This provision for drill was recorded: "Drill yourself on the way to and from school on the multiplication tables." [46:8]

There appeared a statement that the vacation experiences had resulted in an added interest in arithmetic. This will no doubt be capitalized in subsequent curriculum material for that city. As it now stands this course represents, both in content and procedure, a point of view too frequently found in this field. This point of view gives drill for the acquisition of skills precedence over interesting, vital number experiences rich in meanings to the child. Such experience-situations not only extend the child's interests and make further number experiences necessary, but, according to the best current opinion, they form the basis for the most effective drill. The findings for this study showed that the emphasis in the printed curricula was given to associated drill. The statement in this course regarding the interest and improvement in arithmetic resulting from the vacation experiences confirms this point of view. What is needed in this field is fearless and consistent emphasis upon the experiencing of number in lifelike situations appropriate for that particular stage of development of the children concerned. This approach to number not only makes the acquisition of skills necessary to carry on a vital experience, but it provides the dynamic interest for sufficient practice to acquire the needed skill.

Case 6

From the Guiding Point of View. Case 6 reflects a point of view which seems to the writer to represent an inconsistent element in recognized advanced curriculum materials. This case is taken from the results of a curriculum program which has been epoch-making for its leadership in teacher participation and has consistently expressed the philosophy of education as growth. The element in question is reflected in the following point of view for social studies in the upper grades:

Construction work should not be attempted unless there is an expectation on the part of the teacher that it will result in increased understanding. Unless the construction work is a means of elaborating understanding and the time, effort and expense fall within reasonable limits it should not be undertaken. [15:24]

From the Suggested Experiences. It is quite easy to recognize this point of view as a guard against haphazard "doing" and the failure to capitalize the expression of ideas in concrete form by drawing out the necessary associations for making valuable generalizations. However, the underlying possibilities in this area of the industrial arts field merit careful study and much leeway for experimentation.

The influence of the kindergarten has made the expression of ideas in the form of construction an accepted matter for the children of the lower grade levels. The influence of the ability to read for information has been largely responsible for the assumption that concrete experiences were less necessary, or wholly unnecessary, in the upper grade levels of the elementary school. Much observation of the type of construction work which was considered by the pupil-teacher group, or by the individual, as the best medium for the expression of an idea in solving some problem, has assured the writer that this is a rich field for investigation. Gunther's study of "Manipulative Participation" is convincing. More need to follow. The concept of books as the chief source of learning, and the school, especially the upper grades, as a place of quiet, vicarious experiences is a pattern that gives way slowly. Other curriculum materials of the program from which this case was drawn indicate that advance may already be made in solving some of the problems in this interesting area of the contribution of industrial arts to "increased understanding."

A Summary of the Findings from the Application of the Several Guiding Elements

	Per Cent of Materials Examined
I. The Philosophy as Shown in	
1. Statements of the Point of View	43
2. Creeds	11
3. Aims	25
4. Objectives	20
5. Various Plans of Organization	

	Courses
1. Teacher participation in curriculum remaking (as shown in 71 courses and questionnaires)*	

* For information regarding the questionnaire on "Plans of Organization" affecting the curriculum, see pages 36-38.

Cities

a. For a small portion of the total teacher group   21
b. For a fairly large portion of the total teacher
group   35
c. For practically all members of the teaching
staff   15

2. Tests in the so-called subject matter fields
a. Used through a centrally controlled program
to test predetermined subject matter and
results made the chief factor in promotion of
pupils   44
b. Used solely as an instrument of instruction
after recognition by the pupils and teacher
jointly as useful to their needs. The results
given only their relative value in the total
picture of the child's development   27

3. A program of departmentalized instruction.
This was defined as organized upon the basis
of subjects and largely taught by separate
teachers   14

4. A program of instruction organized with one
teacher for each group and largely responsible
for all subjects   16

5. A combination of 3 and 4   4

6. Homogeneous grouping to some degree in so-
called regular classes   Yes   19
                                          No   15

7. An integrated program in which individual differences, except in cases of extreme limitation,
were provided for through a wide range of experiences (Some overlapping here. Reported
as indicated on questionnaire.)   18

II. Building the Personality as a Whole

Per Cent of
Materials
Examined

1. Little or no suggestion of experiences which have been planned to provide opportunities for building the personality as a whole   8
2. Some provision inherent in the suggested experiences, but little emphasis given to opportunities for building the personality   52
3. Definite provision for many wholesome experience-situations which offer rich opportunities for building the personality   39

III. The Place of Environment in Learning

1. No mention of the conscious utilization of the environment   8
2. Utilization of the environment, as found   16
3. Enrichment and utilization of the environment   0
4. A combination of positions of 2 and 3   76

IV. The Curriculum Maker's Theory of the Way Learning Takes Place

1. Learning as training   4
2. Learning as the development of ideas through the assimilation of information   11
3. Learning as a process affecting the human organism in its total experience   49
4. A combination of any of the above positions   35

V. The Place of the Teacher

1. The teacher as a superimposed authoritarian   14
2. The teacher as the most experienced member of the pupil-teacher group   58
3. The teacher as an adviser only in response to request   0
4. A combination of positions   28

VI. The Choice of the Curriculum Experiences

1. Chosen in advance by adults   10
2. A combination of position 1, chosen in advance by adults, and position 2, chosen by teacher and pupils   46

3. Chosen by the teacher and pupils   35
4. A combination of position 2, chosen by the teacher and pupils, and position 3, chosen by the learner   8
5. Chosen by the learner   o

VII. The Relative Immediacy of the Experience to the Child
   1. The experience very remote   18
   2. The experience within the child's mental imaginative environment, through his range of interests and appreciation, but outside his immediate physical environment   11
   3. A combination of position 2, the experience within the child's mental imaginative environment, and position 3, the experience drawn from the child's immediate environment   28
   4. The experience drawn from the child's immediate environment   42

VIII. Provision for Learning through First-Hand Experiences
   1. Little or no provision for first-hand experiences   21
   2. Some provision for first-hand experiences inherent in the suggested outline, but little emphasis given to their use   20
   3. Well-planned provision made for many first-hand experiences in the suggested program   59

IX. Provision for Creative Experience
   1. No recognition or provision for creative experience, as such   28
   2. Some provision inherent in the suggested experiences but little emphasis given to the utilization of these opportunities   30
   3. Definite provision for a rich program of creative experiences   42

X. Growth in Intellectual Curiosity
   1. No provision made, as such   17
   2. Some experiences provided for encouraging intellectual curiosity, but their use not emphasized   57
   3. Many experiences provided for encouraging intel-

lectual curiosity, and emphasis given to their use   25

XI. .Provision for the Enrichment of Leisure Time
1. No provision for the enrichment of leisure time   17
2. Some provision inherent in the suggested experiences, but little emphasis given to the use of these opportunities for the enrichment of leisure time   45
3. Provision for many experiences contributing to the enrichment of leisure time   38

XII. "Socially Useful" Work
1. No provision for "socially useful" work, as such   50
2. Provision for "socially useful" work through the utilization of experiences which are more distinctly physical than social   13
3. A combination of positions 2 and 3   28
4. Provision for "socially useful" work through the utilization of experiences which have an obvious social element   8

XIII. Acquaintance with the National Culture for Appreciation and Improvement
1. Little provision for acquaintance with the national culture, as such   21
2. Some provision inherent in the suggested experiences but little emphasis given to their use for interpreting and judging the national culture   56
3. Many experiences provided and suggestions given for their use in relation to judging and appreciating the national culture   22

XIV. Provision for Growth in World-Mindedness— Building an International Interest
1. Little or no provision for experiences which build interest in other national cultures   29
2. Some provision inherent in the suggested program of experiences, but little evidence of their use in building further interest   52
3. A rich, well-balanced program of suggested experiences with many provisions for building further interest in other cultures   18

XV. Subject Matter: How Thought of and How Accordingly Used
1. Subject-matter-set-out-to-be-learned 17
2. Subject matter largely determined, but enlivened by various activities 27
3. Subject matter as a means to an end 24
4. Subject matter as the total experience 32
XVI. The Place of Drill
1. No drill 13
2. Disassociated drill 22
3. Associated drill 64
4. The need for extra drill reduced (portions of courses under 3 appeared in this position) 0
XVII. The Form Used in Organizing the Curriculum Material
1. A bare topical outline 6
2. An outline, somewhat enriched, of subject matter to be covered 20
3. An elective list ot suggested activities within certain subject matter areas 7
4. An integrated program of experiences 15
5. Units of work 23
6. A statement recommending that the curriculum be "made as you go" 0
XVIII. Some Inconsistencies Between the Philosophy and the Suggested Experiences
The findings for this guiding element are discussed under this heading on pages 161-167.

Chapter IV

TRENDS AS TO APPROVED POSITIONS

THROUGHOUT this study each guiding element has had various positions set up under it to provide for the full range of opinion possible for any curriculum maker to hold and to embody in the printed materials. The approved position set up under each guiding element most nearly reflects the writer's educational philosophy —education as growth through the continuous reconstruction of individual and social experience.

It now seems pertinent to draw out these approved positions and summarize the findings to see how current practice in the selection of curriculum experiences approves or rejects this point of view.

THE APPROVED POSITION FOR EACH GUIDING ELEMENT

Guiding Element Used and the Approved Position

	Per Cent of Materials Approving
I. The Philosophy as Shown in Statements of the Point of View	43
II. Building the Personality as a Whole Definite provisions for many wholesome experience-situations which offer rich opportunities for building the personality	39
III. The Place of Environment in Learning A combination position of Utilization of the Environment, as found, and Enrichment and Utilization of the Environment	76
IV. The Curriculum Maker's Theory of the Way Learning Takes Place Learning as a process affecting the human organism in its total experience	49

V. The Place of the Teacher
The teacher as the most experienced member of the
pupil-teacher group   58
VI. The Choice of the Curriculum Experiences
Chosen by the teacher and pupils   35
VII. The Relative Immediacy of the Experience to the
Child
The experience drawn from the child's immediate en-
vironment   42
VIII. Provision for Learning through First-Hand Ex-
periences
Definite provision made for many first-hand experi-
ences   59
IX. Provision for Creative Experience
Definite provision for a rich program of creative ex-
perience   42
X. Growth in Intellectual Curiosity
Many experiences provided for encouraging intellec-
tual curiosity, and emphasis given to their use   25
XI. Provision for the Enrichment of Leisure Time
Definite provision for many experiences contributing
to the enrichment of leisure time   38
XII. "Socially Useful" Work
A combination of positions 2 and 3, provision for
"socially useful" work through the utilization of ex-
periences which are both physical and have an obvi-
ous social element   28
XIII. Acquaintance with the National Culture for Appreciation and Improvement
Many experiences provided and suggestions given for
their use in relation to judging and appreciating the
national culture   22
XIV. Provision for Growth in World-Mindedness—
Building an International Interest
A rich, well-balanced program of suggested experiences with many provisions for building further international interest   18

XV. Subject Matter: How Thought of and How Accordingly Used
Subject matter as the total experience   32
XVI. The Place of Drill
Associated drill   64
XVII. The Form Used in Organizing the Curriculum
Material. An integrated program of experience (Units
of Work, type b)   23

The purpose of this summary upon which the present chapter is based was to show the per cent of the materials examined which had made provision for the approved position under each guiding element. The extent of the provision, as expressed by the per cent, was not the only question of importance here; but the evidence, however slight, that the elements set up under that particular position had been recognized in printed curricula was also considered of great importance. Attention is here called to the fact that in the courses which made the most provision for these elements, the inter-relationship between the philosophy and the suggested experiences was most apparent. The summary, then, reflects twofold implications. The trends carry an added significance.

It is interesting to note the range in the per cent to which the current curriculum materials provided for the elements embodied under the approved positions. This point is well illustrated by the findings of 59 per cent for the approved position under "Provision for Learning Through First-Hand Experiences," while "Provision for Growth in World-Mindedness," which has received only recent recognition in current literature, appeared in 18 per cent of the materials examined. It seems possible that two influences in the educational field, not specifically mentioned in the guiding elements used in this study, have, no doubt, exerted a marked influence upon the extent to which first-hand experiences were provided for in printed curricula. Reference is here made to the influence of the kindergarten upon the elementary school and the emphasis, of some duration, which has been given to first-hand experiences in current educational literature. This range in the per cent of provision again stands out for associated drill, under "The Place of Drill," with 64 per cent, while the approved position for "Acquaintance with the National Culture for Appreciation and Improvement" shows only 22 per cent. The two guiding elements for which comparatively small provision was made are extremely important to the larger concept of the contribution of education to the total social structure. That these two elements, the one dealing with the national culture, the other, with building an international interest, are now beginning to receive attention, should be noted with satisfaction. It seems reasonable to expect that further needed provision for such important elements will appear in subsequent curriculum materials.

OUTSTANDING TRENDS AS TO APPROVED POSITIONS

The trends here recorded are based upon the preceding summary. They reflect interesting high points embodied in the findings for this study. The most outstanding trends will be noted here. Their deeper implications will appear in the conclusions. The word "Toward" will be used here to suggest a continuing movement rather than a stage arrived at, but the figures given indicate present practice as far as it is revealed by this study.

From	*Toward*
The concept of education for a passive child.	The concept of education based upon experiencing. Provision made for many first-hand experiences: participation; investigation; creativity; enrichment and extension of interests; growth in self-direction.

Certain aspects drawn from a number of the guiding elements used contributed to this trend. Evidence of the trend is especially centered in the findings under the guiding element dealing with "Provision for Learning through First-Hand Experiences." Here 59 per cent of the materials examined recognized its importance. Further sources of evidence were found in the guiding elements dealing with "The Relative Immediacy of the Experience to the Child," "The Place of the Environment in Learning," "Growth in Intellectual Curiosity," "Provision for Creative Experience," and the concept of subject matter as the total experience.

From	Toward
Emphasis upon a subject matter curriculum.	Emphasis upon guiding child growth by means of: a series of experiences which utilize, enrich, and balance the environment. Choice of the curriculum experiences largely by the teacher-pupil group within guiding lines. Experiences planned to build the personality as a whole with the concept of subject matter as the total experience.

Again, the elements reflecting this trend are embodied in several criteria, but evidence of this general tendency is especially reflected in "The Place of the Environment in Learning," "The Choice of the Curriculum Experiences," "Building the Personality as a Whole," and the concept of subject matter as the total experience.

From	Toward
Little relation between subject matter and other experiences.	A guiding point of view applied to the curriculum problem as a whole. Learning as a process affecting the human organism in its total experience. Attention given to encouraging intellectual curiosity and to enriching leisure time. The concept of subject matter as the total experience.

From	Toward
The curriculum experiences wholly determined in advance by adults with a definite body of subject matter set out to be acquired.	The curriculum experiences chosen by the teacher-pupil group with respect to changing guiding elements.

From	Toward
The concept of subject matter as something set out to be learned.	Subject matter as the total experience.

This trend is especially shown in the findings for the guiding element, "Subject Matter: How Thought of and How Accordingly Used." It was stated previously that the size of the per cent was not the sole element here. The fact that 32 per cent of the materials recognized this concept of subject matter is a good omen.

From	*Toward*
The concept of learning as training.	Learning as a process affecting the human organism in its total experience.

The evidence to support this important trend appeared under the guiding element, "The Curriculum Maker's Theory of the Way Learning Takes Place." The findings showed that 49 per cent of the materials recognized this concept of learning as important.

From	*Toward*
Drill given for a possible future use. Disassociated from the need.	Drill associated with the need for a skill to carry out some purpose of the teacher-pupil group. Recognized by the learner as necessary to that end and practiced to serve it.

That the trend toward associated drill is a distinct one is shown under the guiding element, "The Place of Drill," by 64 per cent of the materials examined.

From	*Toward*
The teacher as an authoritarian.	The teacher as the most experienced member of the pupil-teacher group.

This point of view is especially emphasized in the findings for "The Place of the Teacher." Here 58 per cent of the materials examined recognized this point of view as outstanding.

From	*Toward*
Emphasis wholly upon the in-school experiences.	Definite provision for many experiences contributing toward the enrichment of leisure time.

From	*Toward*
Little provision on the extension of interests.	Definite recognition and provision for encouraging intellectual curiosity and the enrichment of leisure time.

From	*Toward*
Little emphasis upon the acquaintance with the national culture. Blind acceptance of institutions and procedure.	Recognition of the need to study the national culture for appreciation and improvement.

From	*Toward*
Little emphasis upon building an international interest.	Recognition of the need to build an attitude for world-mindedness.

From	Toward
Little or no provision made for participation in worth-while work with the community group as American life became urbanized.	Provision for "socially useful" work appropriate for the age level of the child.

Trends of today become the accomplishments of tomorrow and lend their influence toward other trends. Such influences upon subsequent curriculum thought have far-reaching possibilities.

In an examination of the elements of organization which seemed most likely to influence the type of curriculum materials found in the various cities, the following were consistently present in the situations from which the materials in this summary were drawn: (1) The element of teacher participation in curriculum construction appeared to a greater extent in this group than in any of the 71 courses examined. (2) In all the situations represented in the materials of this summary there were provided the continuous services of a person in charge of the problem as a whole. This procedure insured the co-ordination of the many aspects and capitalized all possible contributions to their fullest service.

There was evidence in the courses of this group, and in the questionnaire sent to 34 cities, that a person, or small staff, had concentrated upon the problem for some length of time. There was ample evidence in the most outstanding courses that the person, or persons, who had done the real work of guiding the curriculum had a thorough acquaintance with the underlying principles of current-curriculum thought and the necessary laboratory experience to apply these principles. Only under such conditions could they be capitalized into rich experience-situations for eager, growing children. Both elements are vital to the problem. Without the vision and understanding resulting from this combination, curriculum guidance fails to make its full contribution to the child's total educative process. In the outstanding curricula a too frequent error had been avoided —that of divorcing the curriculum program from its instructional laboratory. Such a divorcement prevents the increment of the one from contributing to the growth of the other. On this vital aspect of curriculum planning Taba says:

> For the sake of the fruitfulness and the integrity of the educational process, it is important that whatever of value has emerged from its experiences at any stage should be consciously utilized in the guidance of the

subsequent experiences. The learning that is to follow . . . should at least be partly determined by the experiences that have preceded, in order that the learning be continuous and fully educative. Consequently, the guidance of such a flowing and evolving process cannot be done quite adequately apart from and prior to, that process, however efficiently it may be done . . . any expert planning of the educational material and processes outside of the immediate practice is liable to cramp learning and limit the creative development of the educative experiences. [72:244]

Chapter V

CONCLUSIONS, RECOMMENDATIONS, AND PROBLEMS FOR FURTHER STUDY

IN THIS study of the relationship of the professed philosophy to the suggested educational experiences the attempt has been made, through the guide devised for the study of the relationship, to approach the problem by seeking important guiding elements rather than through an atomistic analysis of subject matter content. The point of view of any curriculum maker on these guiding elements reveals to a large extent the philosophy which he holds and which should appear in "Statements of the Point of View," "Creeds," "Aims," and "Various Plans of Organization." The consistency with which the philosophy, stated or implied, has been carried out should be revealed by its embodiment in the program of suggested experiences.

The philosophies underlying curricula appear in printed statements, guiding elements, implications, and the organization, equipment, and materials to carry out the proposed educational program. The suggested experiences, if consistent, embody the philosophy. Each of these two major elements is sensitively dependent upon the other in curricula, suggesting a series of ever-widening and meaningful experiences to the learner. Therefore the relationship which exists between them is of vital importance to the curriculum problem as a whole.

CONCLUSIONS WHICH MAY BE STATED WITH A CONSIDERABLE DEGREE OF CERTAINTY ON THE BASIS OF EVIDENCE FOUND

Some of the printed curricula for the period of this study show no statements of a point of view and little evidence of a central guiding philosophy for the problem as a whole. In such curricula the philosophy, or philosophies, reflected by some of the forewords, statements of "subject matter" objectives, organization, and the equipment and materials implied show confusion in the curriculum thinking. It follows that the suggested experiences embody this confusion. Conflicts and inconsistencies exist both between the relationship of the suggested experience to the total curriculum problem and within the various "subject matter" fields.

The printed curriculum materials which show little or no evidence of a central guiding philosophy applied to the problem as a whole, show suggested experiences largely of the traditional, subject-matter-set-out-to-be-learned type.

The printed curriculum materials showing statements of a guiding point of view which was not applied reflect many inconsistencies and little or no relationship between the chosen philosophy and the suggested experiences. The suggested experiences in such courses are largely of the traditional type. The printed curricula which record statements of a guiding philosophy for the problem as a whole and reflect evidence of consistent effort to apply this philosophy to all aspects of the problem, show varying per cents of provision in their materials for the elements incorporated in the "Guide for the Evaluation of Elementary Curricula." The guiding elements used in the approach to the problem of the relationship between the professed philosophy and the suggested experiences were those determined by experts and jury judgment as pertinent to worth-while experience-situations for the growing child. The curriculum maker's point of view on these guiding elements largely reflects the philosophy which he holds.

The provision made for the underlying elements embodied in the guide and the apparent relationship between the guiding philosophy and the suggested experiences *appear together consistently* throughout the curriculum materials examined in this study.

The "Various Plans of Organization" show frequent inconsistencies in the application of the stated guiding philosophy to the curriculum problem. The curriculum materials examined reflect conflicts between the stated guiding point of view and elements within the administrative organization itself. In such situations the inconsistencies reflected in the suggested experiences mount rapidly when viewed in the total curriculum picture. This, unfortunately, remains true when suggested experiences imply learning situations of value which must attempt to function through organization which *limits* rather than *promotes* the educational program. The curriculum materials show that the concept of subject matter is one of the major storm-center areas in the total curriculum problem. The curricula which show the most provision for the underlying elements embodied in the criteria used show the most teacher participation and the continuous guiding services of a person, or a group, having a broad understanding of the principles involved and laboratory experience in the area for which suggestions are being offered.

The per cent of provision, in the curriculum materials for the "chosen position" under various guiding elements, carries important information as a basis for trends. The size of the per cents is not the only element under consideration here. The recognition of a social need, embodied in a new guiding element, is the encouraging factor. In case an advanced sector of classroom procedure reflects that element to a greater per cent than the printed curricula, it should be gratifying. If the condition should be reversed, a point of view stated in print should assist opinion and procedure to coalesce.

"Building the Personality as a Whole" is recognized in printed curricula as important in 39 per cent of the materials examined. This carries valuable implications for the well-rounded growth of the individual.

"Provision for Enrichment of Leisure Time," recognized in 38 per cent of the materials examined, holds many possibilities for the extension of interests. Learning as a process affecting the human organism in its total experience, as the "chosen position" under "The Curriculum Maker's Theory of the Way Learning Takes Place," shows provision made for it in 49 per cent of the materials. This element goes hand in hand with a broader concept of subject matter and the use of drill associated with the need.

The outstanding recognition of "The Place of Environment in Learning" is important and conspicuously inter-related with "The Relative Immediacy of the Experience to the Child." The latter is recognized in 42 per cent of the materials and offers an element of wide implications to the learning experience.

"Provision for Creative Experience," appearing in 42 per cent of the materials, offers deep respect to the individual. The usual concept used for this element is that of "creative expression" and has been largely limited to expression in the field of the arts rather than including thought itself, as creative experience.

"Provision for Learning through First-Hand Experiences" is recognized, in print, as important to the curriculum problem in 59 per cent of the materials examined. It is reasonable to infer that the influence of a philosophy based upon experiencing has played an important role in relation to this element. "The Place of the Teacher" as the most experienced member of the pupil-teacher group received recognition in 58 per cent of the materials. This carries the important implication of wider experiencing and growth in self-direction for the child.

Associated drill, under the guiding element dealing with "The Place of Drill," was provided for in 64 per cent of the materials examined. The association of the need with the practice necessary to acquire a skill in the situation in which it functions, is vital to the total learning experience. Here the two are inextricably bound together in a situation vital to the learner. No subterfuge of "making it interesting" is imposed for lack of inherent interest. Whether this holds true in classroom procedure or not, the declaration of a position is a vantage point toward which procedure may be expected to move. This should be increasingly true as teachers increasingly participate in all aspects of the curriculum problem.

The concept of subject matter as the total experience is recognized as important in 32 per cent of the materials examined. This beginning of a broader concept of subject matter goes hand in hand with associated drill and learning as a process affecting the human organism in its total experience.

Such a guiding element as "Provision for Growth in World-Mindedness," recognized as important in only 18 per cent of the printed curricula, stands out as an urgent need at present. "Acquaintance with the National Culture for Appreciation and Improvement," "Provision for Growth in Intellectual Curiosity," and "Socially Useful Work" are all recognized and give promise of contributing to dynamic curriculum experiences.

There has appeared scattered through the foregoing results some positive evidence to support the following conclusions:

Curricula which make no statements of a guiding point of view for the problem as a whole, largely show traditional subject-matter-set-out-to-be-learned.

Curricula which use subject matter objectives for the total problem show many inconsistencies and the suggested experiences are largely of the subject matter type.

Curricula which state a guiding point of view and *do not apply it* show numerous inconsistencies between the stated philosophy and the suggested experiences.

Curricula which state a guiding point of view for the problem as a whole and show consistent effort *to apply it* reflect more relationship between the professed philosophy and the suggested experiences, to carry it out, than any other type of curriculum here studied. In such curricula the experience-situation suggestion appears more frequently than in any other type.

In general, then, the underlying assumption of this study seems corroborated—When a philosophy of education has been formulated, tentative to be sure, and stated as a central guiding element for the curriculum problem as a whole, its application will promote a more consistent relationship between the guiding philosophy and the suggested experiences than now exists.

RECOMMENDATIONS

On the basis of this study, the following recommendations are made:

A co-operatively determining guiding philosophy arrived at by all persons to whom it applies.

A tentative plan for an educational program to carry out the proposed philosophy. The guiding lines for this program are to be developed by all persons concerned—teachers, children, parents, and other citizens.

The application of the stated guiding philosophy to the administrative organization so that it functions by *serving* rather than *limiting* the proposed educational program.

The proposed educational program is to be concerned with the continuous experimentation and evaluation of tentative guiding lines along which more dynamic experience-situations may be made possible for the growing child. Such a program implies experiencing, planning, choice and responsibility, sharing and enjoying achievements, and increasing self-direction on the part of the learner.

Continuous critical thinking by all persons involved is offered as a guide to insure the fundamental purposes of such an educational program.

PROBLEMS FOR FURTHER STUDY

The following problems are suggested for investigation:

Further study of "Socially Useful" Work appropriate for the child of elementary school age. This investigation is to study possibilities, as well as to build an adult attitude toward the purpose and necessity of such experiences to the child.

Investigations carried on in co-operation with the parents to find what type of experience-situations within the school group lead to worth-while individual and small-group experiences in the home and community groups.

Further investigation of the learning possibilities inherent in more manipulative experiences than are now provided for the child of the upper age levels in the elementary school.

An investigation of the purposes of children when working individually and when stimulated by the group.

Several studies in the field of values accruing from types of curriculum experiences.

A study of what elements constitute a good balance between individual and group experiences for the child at various levels of development.

Further investigation of attitudes and concepts growing out of certain types of curriculum experiences.

Appendix
and
Bibliography

List of Persons Co-operating in "A Study of the Relationship Between the Philosophy and the Suggested Experiences in Recent Printed Curricula for the Elementary School"

Baldwin, Emma, Supervisor of Elementary Grades, San Diego Public Schools, San Diego, California.

Cushman, C. L., Director, Research Department, Denver Public Schools, Denver, Colorado.

Grant, Alice M., Formerly Instructor of Mathematics, Winthrop College, Rock Hill, South Carolina.

Green, Ellen F., Instructor, Department of Education, Fisk University, Nashville, Tennessee.

Ligo, Ida Louise, Instructor in English, High School, New York City.

Piper, Helen J., Supervisor, Grades 4, 5, 6, Lynn Public Schools, Lynn, Massachusetts.

Reynolds, Helen M., Director, Department of Kindergarten-Primary Education, Seattle Public Schools, Seattle, Washington.

Rudy, Ida O., Formerly Primary Supervisor, now Director Social Studies and Elementary School Principal, Dayton, Ohio.

Wickey, Rose, Director, Curriculum Department, Public Schools, Kansas City, Missouri.

APPENDIX II

Statements from Curriculum Makers in Several of the Cities from Which the Materials for This Study Were Drawn

These statements were made in response to a request embodying two elements: (1) Your opinion on the need for a more consistent relationship between the guiding philosophy and the suggested experiences. (2) How your group attained the relationship which is apparent in your curricula.

I

In our curriculum study and revision we believe that true progress ultimately takes place only as all of us concerned with the education of the children reach a similar point of view regarding human values. We believe, also, that this point of view must be interpreted in procedures which are not antagonistic to the philosophy which we profess to accept. We believe further that sometimes we may work our way into a better interpretation of our accepted philosophy through discussion, study, and trial of the procedures of other students of the same problem.

We attempt to reach a common basis for thinking and acting through many different channels, among them these:

1. Frank questioning and discussion of situations arising in the work with the children in our Demonstration School and in all our schools.

2. The study of teaching in the light of accepted statements of philosophy from the writings of Dewey, Kilpatrick, and others.
3. A study of the reactions of boys and girls to life in school as reported by parents.
4. Consideration of the criticism of parents as related to actual conditions for learning.
5. Attempts to continually check procedures suggested or recorded as to whether they are in harmony with purposes or outcomes included in our tentative statements of curriculum.
6. The continuous study of the work of other curriculum committees—their efforts to state goals and to follow ways of working which will lead to ends desired. The study of the skill with which they meet their conditions stimulates openmindedness on our part as to better ways of working out the faith that is in us.
7. Continued efforts at the statement and restatement of the educational principles underlying our work. This effort to formulate ideas goes on in groups large and small in every department of our school life. We consciously work for the clarification of our ideas through discussion and application.

HELEN M. REYNOLDS
Director, Department of Kindergarten-Primary Education
Seattle Public Schools

II

Our various courses of study have been prepared by different committees working independently. While I fully agree that there is a great need for consistency between the guiding philosophy as set forth in any course of study and the suggested experiences outlined in the course, there has been no definite plan followed in Denver in attempting to attain that consistency. The only suggestion that I have is that we must continually ask ourselves and insist that our associates ask themselves what it is we are really trying to do in our school program.

C. L. CUSHMAN
Director, Department of Research, Denver Public Schools

III

A Statement Regarding the Relationship Between the Philosophy and the Suggested Experiences in Curricula

Every person has, not a philosophy, but philosophies; values and standards that serve to guide and evaluate his personal life, his social life, his business life. Teachers have philosophies of education of the school, of the divisions of the school, of different subject fields, of method and procedure. Too frequently these philosophies are lost sight of, and both practice and viewpoints become fixed or static. It is well, therefore, to pause from time to time to extract one's philosophies from his practice, to scrutinize them critically, and to reconstruct them in the light of changing conditions and new values.

In the continuous process of curriculum revision, it is especially essential that philosophies appear and change and grow, for they set the goals of educational endeavor and service as a means of guiding and evaluating practice.

Where curriculum revision is a truly co-operative piece of work, as we believe it is in Kansas City, teachers participate in formulating the underlying philosophy of a course and in suggesting experiences or activities related to this philosophy. The studies teachers make, the experiences they have, the responsibilities they share in curriculum construction, are potent means of producing and improving educational philosophies and suggesting educative experiences in the light of these philosophies.

ROSE WICKEY
Director, Curriculum Department
Public Schools, Kansas City, Missouri

IV

How Our Philosophy Was Developed

Our committee consisting of teachers of outstanding ability, the supervisor of grades one through four, and some principals met to discuss the plans for our Course of Study. All were people who had recently studied modern educational theories, and they knew something about how to proceed. We agreed that no course of study could be launched without a sound philosophy of education to back it up. We immediately set up our criteria for our philosophy and began to evaluate these in terms of the best modern theories of education.

We sifted our evaluations down to very definite principles by which we were to be guided in our experimental work.

We took the position that the "School is Life," where such living and learning are experienced as could not be obtained in any other way. We also concluded that no curricula could consider only the mental life of the child, but that this life plus his emotional and physical life, his aesthetic and spiritual life, which means the whole child had to be taken into account. This of course would call for the study of the individual Child in his many-sided experiences. We also took into serious account that wherever there are children there must be activity, the outcomes of which we felt were to a degree predictable and measurable. We realized that these situations should also provide controlled environment.

Our committee agreed that since the greatest impressions are made during the early years of a child's life, these years should be the time when habits, attitudes and ideals, as well as skills, should be learned through direct and concomitant learnings.

Upon Child life now (meaning today) in our changed living situations, with its interests and tendencies, emphasis was to be placed. We agreed that controls would be gained through the natural settings which the modern and progressive educational plan afforded.

We stressed the need for careful guidance in these activities and experiences which children were to be afforded, and that subject matter must not be considered an end in itself, but as Dr. Kilpatrick has said, "it is a way of behaving learned in the experience." Thus, with this philosophy we set about to work in our various centers and units, attempting to relate these principles closely with the activities and classroom experiences. We held that no course of study could be built up without a sound philosophy, nor could a philosophy be built up without knowledge of what will take place in progressive classroom situations. The two so closely related must be continuous, without even a semblance of a break between.

The Relationship between the Philosophy Set Up and the Actual Experiencing in Classroom Activities

Having agreed definitely upon our philosophy, and guided by these principles, we launched the work in our classrooms. Very definitely we proceeded in the following way.

1. At each stage of development of the child we knew there were certain definite goals to be reached.

2. We set up our goals to meet the needs of each grade group at each stage of development, keeping closely in mind the philosophy which we had set up.

3. Careful direction and guidance led to the "setting of the stage," which would create spontaneous, free, enthusiastic response from the children.

4. Keeping ourselves in the background, stepping in when needed to guide, to restrain (if any serious situation arose) and to bring about a controlled environment, we carried forward the activities of each unit.

5. Our philosophy became interwoven in our activities, and our activities were guided by our philosophies.

6. Each fits into the other, each is necessary to the other, and in this belief, we succeeded in working out units which are included in our curricula for our grades one through four.

All good curricula must be based upon sound philosophy of education. All education must have a sound philosophy as a foundation for all activities. This proved true in our experimental work.

IDA O. RUDY
Formerly Primary Supervisor
now *Director, Social Studies and Elementary School Principal*
Dayton, Ohio

V

The most valuable, far-reaching, and perhaps most difficult, work of the Supervisor is that of interpreting a philosophy of education to teachers through the curriculum. The work of making courses of study is interwoven with the whole fabric of school procedure. If it is a co-operative undertaking, providing for the participation of all those who have the responsibility of carrying out the activities recommended by the curriculum, then it truly becomes one of the best, if not the best, means of giving teachers an insight into educational theory through their own experiences. In other words, we apply the philosophy of "learning through doing" to teachers as well as to children.

In planning a curriculum revision program in Lynn, the first step was to raise the level of teaching procedure to that suggested by courses of study already existing. Then followed the formation of principles more in accord with modern educational theory and an attempt to improve teaching in general through the development of activities more in harmony with the accepted principles. Those teachers who were carrying on more informal types of work were encouraged in this, and invited to demonstrate newer practices to others in their group. All teachers were asked to carry out one unit of study, in any field whatsoever, to keep a record of their aims, procedures, pupil activities, materials used, results they felt were accomplished, and suggestions they would make for future changes. These units were put on file in the Supervisor's offices for the use of all teachers. At demonstrations and at teachers' meetings, the principles underlying these activities were discussed and outcomes evaluated in terms of objectives set up. As teachers planned newer activities in associated fields, they came to see the value of integrated units of study and the work became less formal in many classrooms.

The purchase of more varied materials and equipment helped materially in the problem of freeing the classrooms from formal learning procedures.

Following these activities, a program of curriculum revision was initiated. An elementary curriculum council made up of teachers, principals, and supervisors worked out basic principles as a guide to this work. Then came the organization of the several committees of teachers in the guidance of the supervisors concerned. The experiences they had already gained made for keen interest in the newer problem of organized curriculum construction. As tentative courses of study were prepared, they were tried out for a year to determine the value of the experiences selected.

Integration of allied fields as that of art, music, physical education with social studies proved of valuable help in broadening the teacher's viewpoint.

An important phase of the work has been definite planning for wholesome contacts with community life. For example, such contacts are being made through the study of local history, the text for this study having been written by the pupils themselves.

The extended use of books has led to the organization of a Library Council, now eight years old. This Council meets each month with the Children's Librarian of the Public Library for a program planned to stimulate proper use of our public libraries and their materials. This information reaches all pupils in the intermediate grades through the Council members.

Means employed for initiating curricula have been free discussion of the material at teachers' meetings; demonstrations of activities by committee members; selected teachers asked to try out definite units and report on same; the teacher committee concerned presenting the course to their group and discussion by an expert in the field concerned.

The committees organized in 1928-1930 still function, and continue to produce new material as the need arises.

HELEN J. PIPER
Supervisor, Grades 4-5-6
Lynn Public School, Lynn, Massachusetts

Bibliography

1. ANN ARBOR, MICHIGAN, BOARD OF EDUCATION. *Social Studies Course for Kindergartens and Grades I and II.* 1929. 84 pp.
2. BIRMINGHAM, ALABAMA, BOARD OF EDUCATION. *General Course for the Elementary Grades.* 1933. 15 pp.
3. BODE, BOYD H. *The Educational Frontier.* Edited by William H. Kilpatrick. New York: The Appleton-Century Co., 1933. 325 pp.
4. BODE, BOYD H. *Modern Educational Theories.* New York: The Macmillan Company, 1927. 331 pp.
5. BONSER, FREDERICK G. *Life Needs and Education.* New York: Bureau of Publications, Teachers College, Columbia University, 1932. 288 pp.
6. BONSER, FREDERICK G. *The Speyer School Curriculum.* New York: Teachers College, 1913. 179 pp.
7. BROWN, CORINE. *Creative Drama in the Lower Grades.* New York: D. Appleton and Company, 1929. 210 pp.
8. CAMPBELL, CHARLES MACFIE. *Human Personality and the Environment.* New York: The Macmillan Co., 1934. 252 pp.
9. CHICAGO, ILLINOIS, BOARD OF EDUCATION. *Social Studies Course for Grades I, II, and III.* 1932. 126 pp.
10. CHILDS, JOHN L. *Education and the Philosophy of Experimentalism.* New York: The Century Co., 1931. 264 pp.
11. COUNTS, GEORGE S. *Dare the School Build a New Social Order?* New York: The John Day Company, 1932. 56 pp.
12. CUBBERLEY, ELLWOOD P. *Public Education in the United States.* New York: Houghton Mifflin Company, 1934. 782 pp.
13. DAYTON, OHIO, BOARD OF EDUCATION. *A Suggestive Course of Study for Grade Two.* 1931. 156 pp.
14. DENVER, COLORADO, BOARD OF EDUCATION. *A General Course of Study for Kindergartens and Grades I and II.* 1930. 136 pp.
15. DENVER, COLORADO, BOARD OF EDUCATION. *A Social Studies Course for Grades I and II.* 1932. 127 pp.
16. DENVER, COLORADO, BOARD OF EDUCATION. *A Social Studies Course for Grades 4, 5, and 6.* 1930. 48 pp.
17. DETROIT, MICHIGAN, BOARD OF EDUCATION. *A Course in General Arts.* 1932. 320 pp.
18. DETROIT, MICHIGAN, BOARD OF EDUCATION. *A Course of Study in Arithmetic for Grades Two-Six.* 1930. 245 pp.
19. DEWEY, JOHN. *The Child and the Curriculum.* Chicago: University of Chicago Press, 1902. 40 pp.
20. DEWEY, JOHN. *Democracy and Education.* New York: The Macmillan Company, 1916. 434 pp.
21. DEWEY, JOHN. Editorial. *Social Frontier*, January, 1935.
22. DEWEY, JOHN. *Source Book in the Philosophy of Education.* Edited by William H. Kilpatrick. New York: The Macmillan Company, 1934. 535 pp.

23. DEWEY, JOHN AND CHILDS, JOHN L. *The Educational Frontier.* Edited by William H. Kilpatrick. New York: The Appleton-Century Co., 1933. 325 pp.
24. DUNN, FANNIE W. "Tentative Criteria for Curriculum Selection." *Progressive Education,* October, 1934.
25. FORT WORTH, TEXAS, BOARD OF EDUCATION. *A Course of Study in Arithmetic for Grades 1, 2, and 3.* 1932. 268 pp.
26. FORT WORTH, TEXAS, BOARD OF EDUCATION. *A Social Studies Course for Grade 3.* 1933. 278 pp.
27. FORT WORTH, TEXAS, BOARD OF EDUCATION. *A Social Studies Course for Grade 5.* 1933. 146 pp.
28. GRAND RAPIDS, MICHIGAN, BOARD OF EDUCATION. *An Arithmetic Course of Study for Grades 4, 5, and 6.* 1931. 172 pp.
29. GRAND RAPIDS, MICHIGAN, BOARD OF EDUCATION. *Fine Art Course of Study for Grades 4, 5, and 6.* 1931. 146 pp.
30. GRAND RAPIDS, MICHIGAN, BOARD OF EDUCATION. *A General Course of Study for Grades 2 and 3.* 1930. 2 Vols.
31. GRAND RAPIDS, MICHIGAN, BOARD OF EDUCATION. *A General Course of Study for Grades 4, 5, and 6.* 1931. 3 Vols.
32. GRAND RAPIDS, MICHIGAN, BOARD OF EDUCATION. *A Social Studies Course for Grades 4, 5, and 6.* 1932. 186 pp.
33. HANNA, PAUL R. *Youth Serves the Community.* New York: D. Appleton-Century Co., 1936. 303 pp.
34. JOHNSON, HENRY. *Teaching History in Elementary and High Schools.* New York: The Macmillan Company, 1931. 497 pp.
35. KANSAS CITY, MISSOURI, DEPARTMENT OF EDUCATION. *A Course of Study for the Kindergartens.* 1931. 133 pp.
36. KANSAS CITY, MISSOURI, DEPARTMENT OF EDUCATION. *Social Studies for Primary Grades One, Two, Three.* 1930. 299 pp.
37. KILPATRICK, WILLIAM H. *Education and the Social Crisis.* New York: Horace Liveright, Inc., 1931. 9 pp.
38. KILPATRICK, WILLIAM H. "Certain Conflicting Tendencies Within the Present-Day Study of Education." *Essays in Honor of John Dewey.* New York: Henry Holt & Company, 1929. 425 pp.
39. KILPATRICK, WILLIAM H. *A Reconstructed Theory of the Educative Process.* New York: Bureau of Publication, Teachers College, Columbia University, 1931. 31 pp.
40. KILPATRICK, WILLIAM H. "Tendencies in Educational Philosophies," in *Twenty-Five Years of American Education.* Edited by I. L. Kandel. New York: The Macmillan Company, 1924. 469 pp.
41. KNOXVILLE, TENNESSEE, BOARD OF EDUCATION. *An Art Course for Grades One-Six.* 1933. 25 pp.
42. LEARY, DANIEL B. *Twenty-five Years of American Education.* Edited by I. L. Kandel. New York: The Macmillan Company, 1924. 469 pp.
43. LOS ANGELES, CALIFORNIA. *A Course of Study for Vocation Schools, Grades 3-8.* 1930. 57 pp.
44. MEAD, GEORGE H. *Mind, Self, and Society.* Chicago: University of Chicago Press, 1934. 401 pp.
45. MILLER, H. L. *Creative Learning and Teaching.* New York: Charles Scribner's Sons, 1927. 262 pp.

46. MILWAUKEE, WISCONSIN, BOARD OF EDUCATION. *A Course of Study in Arithmetic for Grades 4-5.* 1931-1933. 52 pp.

47. MOSSMAN, LOIS COFFEY. *Teaching and Learning in the Elementary Schools.* New York: Houghton Mifflin Company. 1929. 202 pp.

48. NATIONAL COUNCIL OF MATHEMATICS TEACHERS. *Tenth Yearbook, Arithmetic in an Activity Program.* New York: Bureau of Publications, Teachers College, Columbia University, 1935. 281 pp.

49. NATIONAL EDUCATION ASSOCIATION. *Department of Adult Education, Addresses and Proceedings,* Vol. 72. Washington, D. C.: National Education Association, 1934. 1006 pp.

50. NATIONAL EDUCATION ASSOCIATION, Department of Superintendence. *Fourteenth Yearbook. Social Studies Curriculum.* Washington, D. C.: National Education Association, 1936. 478 pp.

51. NATIONAL SOCIETY FOR THE STUDY OF EDUCATION. *Twenty-Sixth Yearbook, Part I. Curriculum-Making Past and Present.* Bloomington, Illinois: Public School Publishing Co., 1927. 475 pp.

52. NEWARK, NEW JERSEY, BOARD OF EDUCATION. *A Healthy Personality in the Home, School, and Community.* 1931. 87 pp.

53. NEWLON, JESSE. *Educational Administration as Social Policy.* New York: Charles Scribner's Sons, 1934. 301 pp.

54. NEW YORK CITY, DEPARTMENT OF EDUCATION. *A Course of Study in Art for Grades I-VI.* 1931. 128 pp.

55. OAKLAND, CALIFORNIA, BOARD OF EDUCATION. *A Course of Study in Arithmetic for Grade 1.* 1930. 107 pp.

56. OVERSTREET, H. A. *A Guide to Civilized Leisure.* New York: W. W. Norton & Co., 1934. 257 pp.

57. PITTSBURGH, PENNSYLVANIA, BOARD OF EDUCATION. *A Course of Study in Art for Kindergartens and Grades 1-6.* 1931. 125 pp.

58. PITTSBURGH, PENNSYLVANIA, BOARD OF EDUCATION. *A Social Studies Course for Kindergartens and Grades 1-3.* 1933. 60 pp.

59. PORTER, MARTHA PECK. *The Teacher in the New School.* Yonkers, New York: World Book Company, 1931. 312 pp.

60. RALEIGH, NORTH CAROLINA, SCHOOL COMMITTEE. *A Course of Study for Grades 4, 5 and 6.* 1929. 136 pp.

61. REISNER, EDWARD H. *The Evolution of the Common School.* New York: The Macmillan Company, 1930. 590 pp.

62. RILEY, WOODBRIDGE. *American Thought.* New York: Henry Holt, 1923. 438 pp.

63. ROBBINS, L. H. "The Four H Clubs." *New York Times* Magazine, December 13, 1936.

64. ROCHESTER, NEW YORK, BOARD OF EDUCATION. *A Course in Arithmetic for Kindergarten and Grades 1-6.* 1931. 67 pp.

65. ROCHESTER, NEW YORK, BOARD OF EDUCATION. *A Course of Study for Kindergarten and Grades 1, 2 and 3.* 1931. 36 pp.

66. SAN FRANCISCO, CALIFORNIA, BOARD OF EDUCATION. *An Arithmetic Supplement for Primary Grades.* 1930. 32 pp.

67. SEATTLE, WASHINGTON, BOARD OF EDUCATION. *Social Studies Course for Kindergartens and Grades I, II, and III.* 1930. 435 pp.

68. SHOENFELD, DUDLEY D. "Curiosity as a Symptom." *Child Study,* Vol. 11, December, 1933.

69. SOMMERVILLE, MASSACHUSETTS, SCHOOL COMMITTEE. *A Course of Study for Kindergarten.* 1931. 59 pp.

70. SPRINGFIELD, MASSACHUSETTS, SCHOOL COMMITTEE. *A Social Studies Course for Kindergartens and Grades 1, 2, and 3.* 1930.

71. SUZZALLO, HENRY. *Twenty-five Years of American Education.* Edited by I. L. Kandel. New York: The Macmillan Company, 1929. 469 pp.

72. TABA, HILDA M. *The Dynamics of Education.* London: Kegan Paul, French, Trubner & Co., 1932. 278 pp.

73. TULSA, OKLAHOMA, BOARD OF EDUCATION. *A Course in Arithmetic for Grades 1-4.* 1931. 2 vols.

74. TULSA, OKLAHOMA, BOARD OF EDUCATION. *A Course for Kindergartens.* 1931. 77 pp.

75. VIRGINIA STATE BOARD OF EDUCATION. *A General Course for Grades 1-8.* 1931. 2 vols.

76. WHEELER, R. H. AND PERKINS, FRANCIS T., in *Source Book in the Philosophy of Education.* Edited by William H. Kilpatrick. New York: The Macmillan Company, 1934. 535 pp.

77. WOODWORTH, ROBERT S. *Contemporary Schools of Psychology.* New York: The Ronald Press Company, 1931. 232 pp.